Data Analytics Initiatives
Managing Analytics for Success

The three-axis approach to analytics projects
The categorisation of analytical initiatives could
have already gained and reflect it in our work. Correctly defined categories could
help us to simplify the complexity reasonably and, at the same time, understand the
critical aspects of analytical work. But how can we do it, and what can make it so
complex?

Common attributes of analytics projects
Throughout the book, we reiterate that each analytics project is different. At the same
time, analytics projects have a lot in common, and these features make them unique
compared to other projects. Describing these commonalities could move us further
in the conceptual understanding of analytical work. These specific features impact
the entire project lifecycle, and neglecting them (trying to use general approaches
without tailoring them to analytics projects) can lead to failure.

General ideas of risks and challenges
Challenges and risks — another critical aspect of analytical initiatives that could be
the same from the overall definition perspective, but the realisation and mitigation
could significantly differ based on the previously described project categorisation.

Typical failures and risks per project types
To provide a more tangible point of view, we would like to look at things from the
opposite angle. So far, we have been looking at the typical characteristics of the analytics project (and how to categorise them). We will look at specific types of projects,
provide a high-level assessment of their characteristics from a risk perspective (highly generalised), and comment on the most common problems or challenges.

Typical questions for analytics projects
As the last chapter of the book, we will try to provide you with some examples of
questions that could be asked of relevant people in order to analyse the project. These
questions may help you properly pos5ition the project on to each axis and understand the commonalities and general project challenges. This serves only as an example and may differ a great deal based on your company and environment.

Reviewers:
— Farhaan Mirza, Director of Data Science Research Group
  at Auckland University of Technology
— Elias Castro Hernandez, Technical Program Manager, Machine
  Learning Software Development at UC Berkeley
— Torsten Priebe, Head of Data Intelligence Research Group
  at St. Pölten University of Applied Sciences
— Filip Hlinka; VP of Product, Avast Business at Avast
— Jiří Kacerovský; Chief Data Officer, Head of Data CoE at Komerční banka

Editors: Iva Vávrová, Megan Bedell
Design: Janek Dočekal

Data Analytics Initiatives
Managing Analytics for Success

Ondřej Bothe
Ondřej Kubera
David Bednář
Martin Potančok
Ota Novotný

CRC Press is an imprint of the
Taylor & Francis Group, an **informa** business

AN AUERBACH BOOK

First edition published 2022
by CRC Press
6000 Broken Sound Parkway NW, Suite 300, Boca Raton, FL 33487-2742

and by CRC Press
4 Park Square, Milton Park, Abingdon, Oxon, OX14 4RN

CRC Press is an imprint of Taylor & Francis Group, LLC

ISBN: 978-1-032-30240-9 (hbk)
ISBN: 978-1-032-20851-0 (pbk)
ISBN: 978-1-003-30408-1 (ebk)

DOI: 10.1201/9781003304081

Typeset in Sirba and Soleil
by Janek Dočekal

"By 2023, more than **50%** of D&A strategies will fail to achieve wide-scale adoption, not because of architectures or skill sets, but due to a lack of internal communities."

Gartner®, "Self-Service Analytics Governance With Microsoft Power BI", Georgia O'Callaghan, Joseph Antelmi, August 11, 2021.

"Optimizing value from data and analytics is a **continuous** process. It's not just a once a year activity, it's not just a quarterly activity — you need to think about it as central to everything else that you manage."

Gartner Press Release, "Gartner Data and Analytics Summit India- Day 2 Highlights", August 5, 2021 [https://www.gartner.com/en/newsroom/press-releases/2021-08-04-data-and-analytics-summit-india-day2-conference-highlights].

"Through 2025, **80%** of organizations seeking to scale digital business will fail because they do not take a modern approach to data and analytics governance."

Gartner, "Predicts 2021: Data and Analytics Strategies to Govern, Scale and Transform Digital Business", Saul Judah, Andrew White, Svetlana Sicular, Lydia Clougherty Jones, Guido De Simoni, Ted Friedman, Mark Beyer, Jorgen Heizenberg, Sally Parker, December 2, 2020.

"By 2024, **80%** of technology products and services will be built by those who are not technology professionals, according to Gartner, Inc."

Gartner Press Release, "Gartner Says the Majority of Technology Products and Services Will Be Built by Professionals Outside of IT by 2024", June 14, 2021. [https://www.gartner.com/en/newsroom/press-releases/2021-06-10-gartner-says-the-majority-of-technology-products-and-services-will-be-built-by-professionals-outside-of-it-by-2024].

"By 2023, **60%** of organizations will compose components from three or more analytics solutions to build business applications infused with analytics that connect insights to actions."

Gartner, "Predicts 2021: Analytics, BI and Data Science Solutions- Pervasive, Democratized and Composable", Austin Kronz, Afraz Jaffri, Joao Tapadinhas, Julian Sun, Gareth Herschel, January 5, 2021.

Table of Contents

Part one — The Framework Definition

1   The three-axis approach to analytics projects   21

5 Typical questions for analytics projects 147

Acknowledgement

This book was written thanks to the support of the Data & Business platform and long-term institutional support of research activities by the Faculty of Informatics and Statistics, Prague University of Economics and Business (IP400040).

Foreword

It is my pleasure to have the opportunity to introduce this book via this foreword. For years at UC Berkeley, we have been fortunate to be able to contribute to courses that mix analytics, data science, design, and innovation processes resulting in a large-scale, holistic, data-related skill-base.

A transition has occurred in the world. In the past, research and commercial projects in many areas have relied on deductive logic and a closed form of mathematics. With recent trends in computing, a growing volume of data, and analytics tools, we now have the ability to add inductive and empirical analysis to these projects. This trend dramatically increases our ability to learn, understand, and develop new types of results.

Analytics projects deliver the next-generation applications that transform businesses, generate value, and gain a competitive advantage. Analytics is becoming much more accessible to companies and business users. But, it is necessary to realize that the critical success factors for analytics projects are different from what we knew for classical software development projects. We can find that experiences are limited to our focus, and what could look like a new technology does not necessarily solve all challenges. This is mainly due to their overall complexity that is not connected with the analytical problems but with the overall analytics solution ecosystem.

While many books focus on data science itself, this book contributes to a very important need, which is the ability to manage these types of data-oriented projects. This book also takes the very effective approach of learning to focus on the problem definition, project categorization as well as examples of potential risks and failures on typical analytics projects first instead of focusing first on the technical tool. This problem/solution-driven approach is well known to be successful. In contrast, the alternative approach leads only to an ineffective process of technology looking for a problem.

Once again, congratulations to the authors (Ondřej Bothe, Ondřej Kubera, David Bednář, Martin Potančok and Ota Novotný) for going beyond the topics of ML, AI, and reporting, to fill these important project-oriented aspects of data science.

Ikhlaq Sidhu
Faculty Director & Chief Scientist
Sutardja Center for Entrepreneurship & Technology
UC Berkeley

Looking at the trends of data-related solutions throughout time, we can identify two major phases: a phase of data-driven collection and gathering of information and a phase of data analytics. Some years ago, when computer systems were still new, information was kept on paper or other forms. In those days, the goal of data-related solutions was to capture as much information as possible in a computer system. This led to the emergence of databases and relational database systems.

In recent years, however, the trend has changed. Nowadays, databases are everywhere. In every business and function, there are tons of data stored as files and databases. It is the age of data analytics. The challenge is to integrate the data, analyse it, explore it, find anomalies or patterns, and propose changes based on those patterns. The age of data analytics started with reporting and data warehouse concepts and continues with data science and AI terminologies.

Data analytics is a big area. There are a plethora of books, articles, and videos about it already, each covering a particular aspect of data analytics. For a data analytics project to be successful, different components must be involved. It helps if you have the expertise, an understanding of principles and concepts, a familiarity with the technology tools and services, and control of the project overall.

This book looks at data analytics from the project management point of view. It starts with considerations and aspects of a data analytics project and works its way through the risks, challenges, and pitfalls of an analytics solution. Although this is not a technical book, reading it is helpful for anyone who pursues a career in the data analytics field. Before you face the challenges of an analytics project, you have to know the essential aspects, challenges, and pitfalls.

We have been in data analytics for many years and have helped many customers with their challenges at RADACAD. From our point of view, having a good view of the data analytics project is an essential part of a successful implementation.

Leila Etaati
Microsoft AI and Data Platform Most Valuable Professional
Consultant, Co-Founder
RADACAD

Reza Rad
Microsoft Data Platform Most Valuable Professional
Consultant, Co-Founder
RADACAD

About the Authors

Ondřej Bothe

Ondřej has spent his whole life working in analytics. He has worked in many different roles: from hands-on developer to manager leading a team responsible for project implementation and IT analytical landscape operation. He was on the customer side, receiving advice from a consultant, but he has also worn the consultant hat, advising clients on analytical issues across sectors. Thanks to his economic background, he has a unique view of analytical projects. He can combine the aspect of technology, the delivery approach, and an understanding of data with an economist's perspective to ensure the best possible results for analytical insight consumers. Ondrej graduated from the University of Economics in Prague. Outside of his standard career, Ondrej has worked as a tutor for various educational programmes organized by different entities.

Ondřej Kubera

Ondřej has spent most of his career in IT delivery and consulting, focusing on analytics, including areas such as business intelligence, information management, and data governance. He is passionate about bridging the gap between the business and technical perspectives in the data analytics domain. He graduated from the Czech Technical University in Prague and has experience from a variety of hands-on engineering, as well as client-facing and managerial roles. He has led, designed, and consulted analytics initiatives in major consulting firms, a boutique data intelligence company, and a global pharma company. Most of his analytics projects were international.

David Bednář

David loves data and its presentation, and he has spent most of his career in the analytics area. He benefits from experience from both the academic and the business spheres, where he works on projects that further develop his robust technological background. He is a person who likes to develop anything new and innovative, who can define new architectures and patterns, or lead young talents to growth. David graduated from the Technical University of Ostrava focusing on data management and custom data structures, where he helped with research of multidimensional data structures as a member of the Database Research Group. He has worked for international companies as a business intelligence consultant or architect, mainly focusing on improving solutions with the help of new methods and principles.

Martin Potančok

Martin supports data-inspired decisions in commercial and research projects. He has experience in software development and analytics. He has worked as a business analyst and project manager on software projects delivering mainly budgeting and reporting systems for international companies. Recently, he has been working as a business analyst on data and analytics projects. At the Prague University of Economics and Business, he is in charge of data activities and research projects organized in cooperation with the Faculty of Informatics and Statistics. Specifically, he has been part of the team organizing the Data Festival, Data & Business activities, and projects to expand business capabilities using IT and analytics. He received the Josef Hlávka Award in 2015 and holds a PhD in Applied Informatics from the Prague University of Economics and Business.

Ota Novotný

Ota has over twenty years of practical experience in data and business analytics. He helps people understand the importance and principles of data analytics in both academic and business projects and shows them how to use them in their professional lives. He has already supported thousands of people, helping them familiarize themselves with this modern and increasingly promising area of interest, and a large proportion of them have chosen data analytics as their career path. He is always looking for new ways to harness the potential of data and the associated data analytics for modern business. He is the author or co-author of a number of books, conference papers, and articles in professional journals. Since 2015, he has also devoted his time to the xPORT Business Accelerator, a modern startup business centre at the Prague University of Economics and Business. He has been awarded the Associate Professor degree, as well as a PhD in Informatics at the Prague University of Economics and Business, where he defended his thesis related to the role and deployment of data analytics in corporate governance.

Introduction

The analytics project paradox

We have been wondering why a lot of data analytics projects fail. We see it all around us – either end-users do not accept the results, the solution created is not manageable from a long-term perspective, or there are funding issues after the first project stage. From a certain point of view, there is no good reason for it. There should be enough experience with delivery since "data analytics projects" are not a new discipline (analytics projects have already been the centre of focus for a couple of years). New delivery methods have emerged (specifically, Agile methodology could influence delivery significantly), but this should not have such a substantial impact. Moreover, there should be enough experienced resources on the market to deliver specific analytics solutions, so it should be possible to find technically/analytically oriented people for the projects – not to mention universities with data/analytics focus programmes.

On the other hand, analytics projects are typically highly complex, and this complexity may be hidden and must be considered. The understanding of the user journey, user flow, analytics tasks, and even analytics methods that could be applied is constantly evolving. This complexity could be easily hidden at the beginning of the project. Additionally, the environment is evolving rapidly – specifically, the technological environment makes significant progress every year. For example, we can look at the self-service advanced analytics toolset, at the embedded advanced analytics capability available in standard reporting toolsets or at the computation power in the cloud.

We believe that analytics project failure is, surprisingly, caused by a combination of both factors described above. In general, there are many experts in the data analytics area – as there are many people who talk about analytics, study analytics at university and do some specific part of analytical work as their daily jobs (probably everyone creates reports, and nearly everyone has done a basic statistical calculation at some point). Each of these people has a different perspective and different experiences with a different focus. Furthermore, each of them can provide a singular point of view based on their experience (both technical and business) with running the project. Each of them will be right from some perspective. The challenge is choosing an approach based on the given situation and the environment.

This brings us to the complexity – every analytics problem will be different and need to be solved differently. The fact that we did something in the past does not mean that the same approach will be valid again. From the project success perspective, it does not matter why. As there are many experts in specific analytical areas, there are not that many people who can cover the overall analytics landscape – as this becomes a multidisciplinary problem, which requires a great deal of experience from various areas: IT, data governance, or for example, the analytics journey. The experts in one area can usually solve very complex problems – but only within the area they specialize in. As such, you can easily end up blindly following in one direction that made perfect sense in the beginning but became more complicated later (but usually not impossible). As an example, we can mention graph databases. They are a great and robust tool for specific business problems/questions. They may be used quite successfully for some other analytics tasks as well – with the problem of scaling and flexibility. The problem is fitting graph databases into the analytics ecosystem and drawing a boundary with different analytical approaches. For this, you need to have someone who understands the general data analytics ecosystem and experts for every single component, open-minded and ready to have a pragmatic discussion.

Our approach

We have been working on many analytics projects, and we are big "fans" of this "discipline". That is the main reason we decided to summarize our experiences and create this book, which should primarily help you understand the complexity of the analytics project. When we thought about how to write it, we agreed that the best way to present the complexity was to highlight potential problems and issues. From some perspectives, it is not essential to know what usually goes well; it is better to be more prepared for risky areas and potential project failures. As a result of this approach, the text below might sometimes look negative, focusing on challenges and common mistakes. Believe us, delivering an analytics project is fun; we like doing it, there are many ways of doing it right, and it is definitely possible. It is also not easy – as it is with anything else when you want good results. So please view this book as a description of what may happen – which does not mean that it will happen, especially if you are aware of it. When you are aware of potential challenges, you should be able to mitigate the risks better and thus ensure better delivery.

This book describes analytics project categorization and examples of potential risks and failures on typical analytics projects. The problem is that they may differ in various types of organizations (small companies, large companies) where the company level of analytics maturity and analytics project capabilities may vary wildly. We summarize our knowledge based on our many years' experience of building analytical initiatives and analytical capabilities in our careers on the most general level, which we believe may be helpful.

We hope you can gain a new point of view on analytics projects or at least expand your current one. You may need to think outside of the box. Sometimes, you will probably not agree with us, which may be because your experience differs, or we (you) are used to operating in a different landscape. If this happens, try to think about the bigger picture. Try to view the issue from a different perspective and imagine a completely different project (than the one you are involved in) and a different market environment (than you know). Maybe you will find that this approach will clarify your perspective. It does not mean that what you are doing is wrong – it could potentially show you that there are different ways to operate in the case of a different landscape.

Unfortunately, this book cannot be a "silver bullet" for how to run analytics projects. It is more about helping you realize the complexity that is sometimes hidden. This realization should lead to better results in your day-to-day work on analytics projects. Additionally, it will prepare you for changes caused by external factors or changes caused simply by the natural development of the solution you are working on.

As there can be many perspectives, we will appreciate any feedback, points of view, information on things that might be missing, or just suggestions for improvement. Please feel free to contact us via the following website:

www.successinanalytics.com

The focus of the book

Our goal in this book is to look at the initiation phase of the analytics project, i.e., the project definition, scoping and planning, even before the project start (Figure 0.1). This does not necessarily mean only the real project start, but any project increment, which could shift the analytics goal because of the need for a new scope or approach.

Figure 0.1: The focus of this book is on the initiation phase of analytics projects

The structure of the book

The book is structured into two parts (Figure 0.2). In the first part of the book and Chapter 1 The three-axis approach to analytics projects, we would like to focus on external factors (meaning "outside of the project") that influence the project definition and frame the project scope to avoid as many misunderstandings as possible. Understanding the external environment should help us with both challenges described at the beginning. It should help us understand (and categorize) the complexity of the project, and it should also help us lead a discussion with everyone (from stakeholders to the technical team) to collect all the input framing the different points of view on the analytics work itself. As a result, we should (ideally) end up with a clearly articulated project scope and a consensus on expectations with the stakeholders. Furthermore, when we mention scope, we mean not only the analytics scope but also the "technical" and "data" scopes. This should help us identify the general types of projects with different characteristics.

The first part of the book provides a foundation and structured framework, which is leveraged in the second part. The second part of the book consists of four chapters. In Chapter 2 Common attributes of analytics projects, we would like to look at the commonalities of the analytics project-specific attributes we should always keep in mind (regardless of the type of analytics we are dealing with). These commonalities should be the same across most analytics, but they should be managed differently. This part aims to provide additional insight into the concepts from the first part of the book.

Chapter 3 General areas of risks and challenges is about the most significant risks and challenges connected with the analytics project delivery. It is good to be aware of them as this is the best way to take the mentioned areas into account.

Chapter 4 Typical failures and risks per project types focuses on concrete examples of project types – so it is a reverse point of view. We would like to show the risks (and potential failures) connected with various types of analytics based on the project categorization (from the first part) and common characteristics (from the second chapter of the book).

We have also included questions that could help you fit your project into the context (Chapter 5 Typical questions for analytics projects).

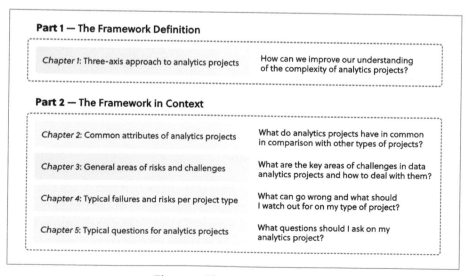

Figure 0.2: The structure of the book

Target audience

We welcome all readers: Stakeholders may use this book to identify the risks and challenges and gain a complex overview of building analytics projects. Delivery leads may use the input in timely risk mitigation and avoiding failures to deliver analytics projects successfully. Data professionals may benefit from the information on project categorization, the differences between projects, and identifying potential risks. Product Owners may use it to understand the specifics of analytics projects. Simply put, this book is for everyone who would like to look at the analytics project from a bird's-eye view and understand the complexity of the work. The greatest benefits to the readers lie in understanding the basic principles of analytical work, which may not necessarily be evident at first sight. Although you may be an expert in one specific area, you can still "get lost" in another one. The challenges of analytical work may be hidden in dependencies and the differences within various analytical steps or subtasks that need to be done to successfully deliver the overall analytical insight. So, this book is for everyone who would like to understand this complexity. Anyone who would like to go one step further, from specialization to generalization, will find this book useful.

Enjoy reading this book; we hope it will support you on your analytics journey.

Part one
The Framework Definition

1 The three-axis approach to analytics projects

The categorisation of analytical initiatives could help us leverage the knowledge we have already gained and reflect it in our work. Correctly defined categories could help us to simplify the complexity reasonably and, at the same time, understand the critical aspects of analytical work. But how can we do it, and what can make it so complex?

As we mentioned at the beginning, many data analytics projects have been delivered. What we have been thinking about, therefore, is how to leverage the experience they yielded – any lessons learned that could help avoid any type of failure in the future. Once again, we would like to emphasize that we are focusing on project external factors only. Due to this, issues like inexperienced delivery teams are not our focus for now. That being said, we have seen many commonly repeated mistakes that lead at least to complications if not to the project's failure. After all, the definition of failure could vary, on a scale of stopping the project entirely to using analytics results insufficiently.

Moreover, we believe that many mistakes could be avoided by investing time at the beginning of the project into understanding the project scope and external landscape. Many things are not easily visible (or could be left out intentionally) or deprioritized for the sake of a speedy delivery (or the start of the project). We realize that discussing this in advance is challenging or might not even be considered agile. Still, we believe that it is one of the critical success factors and should be part of the initiation phase of every data analytics project.

The result of such a discussion should be the categorization of the analytics project. The question is what categorization means. The desired outcome is to understand all (or most) aspects of the project from as many perspectives as possible.

We tried to summarize one of the possible approaches in the following chapters. The text aims to guide the reader through the different views on the analytics project, describe the main questions that should be asked and ideally also answered (or at least considered as a potential risk) or even explain some fundamental failures that could occur. Before we jump in, we need to understand that no analytics project is the same as another. Therefore, we need to try to avoid bias based on our experience and answer questions as openly as possible. This approach could even lead to innovating our way of working (WoW).

To describe this way of thinking, we will try to follow the "three-axis approach". We tried to summarize the different points of view on the analytics project and split various perspectives into three main areas – analytics maturity, IT maturity, and data maturity. We will dive deeper into every area separately, but it is essential not to lose the overall vision. Keep in mind that the combination of the axes is critical. There is no bad or good position on one single axis. What is important is the combination of axes and understanding whether the desired project goal can be delivered easily within the defined combination or whether the expectation (on any level) or the position on any axis needs to be changed.

Moreover, the bigger picture needs to be considered. We focus mainly on the project (whether it is delivered within the waterfall or agile methodology). However, we also need to understand the analytics solution and landscape (this will mainly show in the analytics maturity introduction, but it is also valid for other axes).

The axes do not cover everything. Other aspects are closely connected with the analytics project categorization initially, but even more so with the project/product lifecycle. We will spend some time on these at the end of the book (an example would be a continuous funding challenge).

A project may benefit from following these three axes in a specific order. In any case, you can also leverage this and evaluate your general analytics environment with a focus on one aspect. The recommended "mind flow" is as follows:

Analytics Maturity → Data Maturity → IT Maturity

The reasoning behind this is simple. First, we need to understand what type of analytics we are focusing on. This could significantly influence the required data (it does not necessarily have to be about the data source; for example, the granularity could differ). Later, as soon as we understand the data needed, we can look at the toolset (because it does not necessarily cover only the analytics toolset; steps may also be required just to process/prepare the data for the analytics task itself).

1.1 Axis 1: Analytics Maturity

When it comes to analytics maturity, numerous points of view already exist. The different approaches are often visualized in the form of a chart with various axis definitions (Figure 1.1).

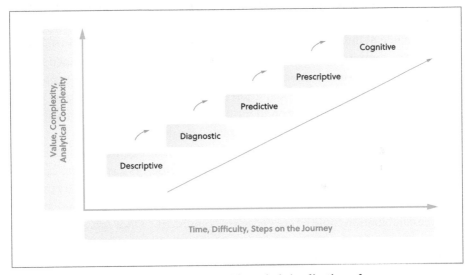

Figure 1.1: Aggregation of the typical visualizations of analytics maturity and the analytics journey

In almost all cases, the "analytics maturity" description is combined with other metrics. Analytics maturity is commonly described as consisting of the following steps:

1. **DESCRIPTIVE**
   It describes, summarizes, and analyses historical data to answer the question "what happened?".

2. **DIAGNOSTIC**
   Based on descriptive analytics, it focuses on the causes, answering the question "why did it happen?".

3. **PREDICTIVE**
   It focuses on the future. Based on available data from the past, it tries to answer the question "what could happen?".

4. **PRESCRIPTIVE**
   It builds on predictive analytics, with an emphasis on recommending the right and optimal solutions or decisions. It answers the question "what should be done?".

5.   COGNITIVE
Incorporating previous types of advanced analytics into autonomous systems with a purely data-driven approach supports independent monitoring, decision making, and action. For this reason,
some approaches include this category in the previous one. This type
of analytics often answers the question "how to adapt to change?".

It is quite understandable that this describes the complexity of an analytical problem. Yet, the definition of "complexity" can be misleading. Is it the complexity
of implementation, the complexity of understanding the business result or the
complexity that impacts implementation time? Is it also necessary that an earlier
step is finished before we move on to the next one – meaning that before starting
a diagnostic project, we need to have completed the descriptive one?

A combination with a second metric could even bring more confusion into
this. One of the commonly used combinations is "value". Is it really the case that
cognitive projects generate the most value? Is a "cognitive project" really the gold
standard for every single area? And is it possible to implement it at any time? Another
possible combination could be created with "complexity". Once again, what makes
the cognitive project the most complex one? Is it really true that predictive projects
are more complex than descriptive ones? And what is the measure of complexity
– is it the implementation time, any other costs connected with the project, or the
experience that the analytics team needs to have?

We have decided to shift the point of view a little. We believe that this project
categorization is correct and should be used. However, we want to look at it through
the lens of the work that needs to happen. So, the first question is: "What is the business goal of the project?" If we can answer it, can we write it down? We need to be
as specific as possible since we need to know the two main features of this work:

1.   Is it project- or solution-oriented?
2.   Is it ad-hoc or robust?

If we find that what we are talking about is the solution, we can consider dividing the
work into more projects. However, this may not necessarily be an effective way to
deal with the issue from a project management perspective. We can evaluate different parts separately, but we usually need to "compose" everything back together
later. The importance of the "solution versus project" consideration lies in something else, however: we need to understand whether there are any hidden parts that
need to be dealt with in order to satisfy the end-user. Therefore, we might start with
a scope that is defined as predictive, but to carry that out in an efficient manner, we
also need to create reports and integrated data. We therefore identify that the original requirement is a solution that can be subdivided into three projects – predic-

tive, reporting, and data integration. This will help us understand and manage the complexity. Try to answer the following questions:

— To what analytics solution, product, or service
  does your analytics project contribute?
— Which other elements of the analytics landscape play an important role
  in the case of your project? Which stakeholders, market conditions, etc.?

Let us have a look at some questions that could help us define the analytics scope:

Q: "What is the business goal of the project?"
A: "To have a sales prediction delivered within the next two months."

This may look like an easy question, but unfortunately, there are many decisions that we cannot make since the answer may have many hidden components. We can use an additional question to clarify:

Q: "Has reporting been established in order to monitor sales?"
A: "Yes."

Q: "Has a plan for sales been set up?"
A: "Yes."

Q: "Should we just try to make the prediction to
   demonstrate it is possible with the available data?"
A: "Yes."

Q: "Should we create a repeated framework for a prediction
   that will be run regularly?"
A: "No."

Q: "How should we share the outputs?"
A: "Presentation."

Q: "Should we integrate the results of the prediction
   into some other system?"
A: "No."

Q: "What is the timetable of the prediction?"
A: "1 year."

The answers to the questions above will probably move us closer. The business goal could then be: "We would like to test a predictive mechanism for sales." We want to test it on actual data and plan sales numbers for one year. This is not a repeated task; the main goal is to see whether this is even possible. Further integration with another system is not needed. If you think about it, changing the answer to any one question could mean a major change for the project's focus (not from a business perspective, but the perspective of the implementation effort and focus). So, for example, if we need to integrate the result into the current system, we must deal with the integration itself, but also the regular prediction calculations, including model management.

Sometimes, it may look as if we are challenging the business problem or even going into technical detail before the project's start. However, these discussions need to happen in every project and having them at the beginning will save everyone a great deal of time and, more importantly, help set the right expectations.

We can move forward as soon as we have a problem definition and understand the type of analytics (project or solution) and the time frame (ad-hoc or robust).

We believe that as part of the analytics maturity question, we need to understand the three main perspectives on the external environment, in addition to the problem definition as such:

1.   Stakeholder analytics maturity
2.   Company analytics maturity
3.   Analytics landscape maturity (both company and solution)

TRY TO ANSWER THE FOLLOWING QUESTIONS:
☐   *To what analytics solution, product, or service*
    does your analytics project contribute?
☐   *Which other elements of the analytics landscape play an important role in*
    the case of your project? Which stakeholders, market conditions, etc.?
☐   *Do you have reports at your disposal?*
☐   *Do you have data at your disposal regularly?*
☐   *Are any additional insights generated automatically? How?*
☐   *Have you established a planning process?*
☐   *Which metrics are regularly planned?*
☐   *Is there any automation in the planning process?*
☐   *How do you address potential future problems? Is it mainly an expert*
    decision? Which support techniques does management have?
☐   *Are the support techniques embedded into the regular reporting process?*
☐   *Do reports contain any recommendations for future steps?*
☐   *Are you able to describe how recommendations are generated/provided?*
☐   *Do you trust the recommendations? Are the recommendations*
    a mandatory part of the planning process?

1.1.1   Stakeholder Analytics Maturity

For this type of maturity, we evaluate whether direct stakeholders can leverage the results. This can be approached from many angles, but in general, it means the following: Does the environment make it possible to use the results and implement them into the business processes of a given department? It is not necessarily only about the "authority of direct stakeholders"; it could also be about the trust in analytics results, especially if they mean unpopular changes to existing processes.

There could be many reasons to run an analytics project, and not all of them are because the analytics results will be used. Let us share some examples:

—   We would like to prove that what we are doing now is right, but we do not want to change if the project results in different recommendations than we expected.
—   We would like to look innovative because others are doing the same.
—   We would like to be recognized as leaders, even though we are followers.
—   We need to prove we are innovative, so we are forced to run a project like this.
—   We are just "in love" with analytics, and we are really dedicated. However, there is no valid business case for the project, or perhaps not even the possibility of implementing the results.
—   We are forced to do it because a higher authority set it as a strategy.

Understanding stakeholders' motivations is vital since we can change the analytics scope or type based on them. For example, if there is no potential for any real change, it could still be valuable to do an ad-hoc project to prove its potential. Alternatively, we can try to use the most advanced analytics method even though we have skipped the previous steps on the analytics journey. This way, we can make minor tweaks in the project definition to save both money and time and improve customer satisfaction or the client's reputation – both of which may be a valid business case from some perspectives.

One specific dangerous scenario might happen, which is mainly valid in the first option where we would like to prove what we are doing through analytical work. The shortest and easiest way NOT to leverage analytics results is to say that there is no trust in the analytics result itself due to wrong methodology or project inputs. That is significantly easier for innovation-led projects or projects with complex algorithms. We might say that what we really want to evaluate is whether the project is even set up for success or not, from a direct stakeholder perspective.

■ **TRY TO ANSWER THE FOLLOWING QUESTIONS:**
- ☐ *How do you gain insight into the business situation?*
- ☐ *Do you have a standard way of analysing your business?*
- ☐ *How much time do you need to update your insight? Is the insight even updated automatically? Are you willing to invest in automation? Does it even make sense?*
- ☐ *Have you ever asked for a prediction of any metrics?*
- ☐ *Have you ever implemented prediction results into the business process?*
- ☐ *Do you use any predictions repeatedly?*
- ☐ *Do you believe in advanced analytics methods? Are you ready to automatize some decisions entirely based on the algorithm recommendation?*
- ☐ *Do you think that human expertise is always needed to make a decision?*
- ☐ *Do you think that a human always needs to double-check automated decisions?*

1.1.2   Company Analytics Maturity

This type of maturity functions basically as the previous type but with a wider perspective. We may still have a direct stakeholder buy-in, but the broader stakeholders can veto any decision. The results of analytics projects could mean a change to a strategy that may not always be overseen by one person or that might require cooperation with other departments, which may have a different maturity level. There also needs to be a good level of confidence that the analytics results will be used in the future. For example, the analytics solution could recommend releasing 50% of the sales force. If we have the buy-in, are we also sure that we will have the same buy-in from the others if the analytics results show that we need to hire 10 new people into the sales force? This is more about the company strategy: is the company generally ready to follow the analytics journey?

If that is not the case, we might need to consider re-evaluating the focus of analytics projects and test their feasibility on a smaller scale or evaluate whether to even start the initiative at all.

■ **TRY TO ANSWER THE FOLLOWING QUESTIONS:**
- ☐ *In your perspective, is the company data-driven?*
- ☐ *Would you categorize your company as innovative?*
- ☐ *Is the analytics solution category a regular part of the budget?*
- ☐ *If you provide enough data, can you achieve a budget increase?*
- ☐ *Are you willing to shift parts of your budget into different departments based on the analytics results (because you can be sure that the reverse will also happen in the future)?*
- ☐ *How would you compare your company with the market from an analytical perspective?*

☐ *Did any disruption occur in the recent past concerning analytics in the industry?*
☐ *Do you have a dedicated data/reporting team?*

1.1.3 Analytics Landscape Maturity

Theoretically, any combination of type of analytics and time frame is valid and can be represented by an analytics project (see Figure 1.2).

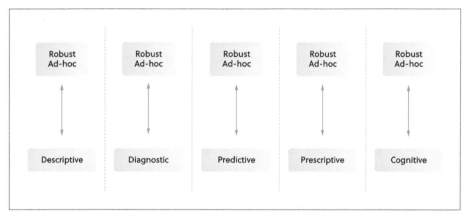

Figure 1.2: There can be ad-hoc and robust projects in any type of analytics

However, does it make sense to implement a robust prescriptive project if we do not have a robust descriptive solution in place? We can find an exception to this rule, but it is usually better to go step by step when it comes to a robust solution. Naturally, these steps may have a different level of complexity for different business areas. For example, does it make sense to have a regular prediction if there are no actual metrics we monitor regularly? What kind of decisions will we be able to make, and how will we evaluate the decisions if we do not have a regular monitoring system (a descriptive solution)? The evolution of the analytics solution is illustrated in Figure 1.3.

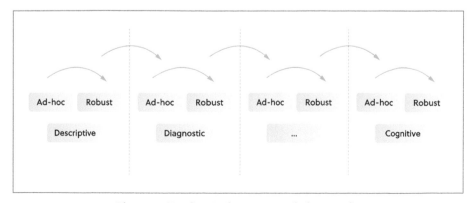

Figure 1.3: Step-by-step journey on analytics maturity

An additional area we can evaluate as part of the analytics landscape maturity is a comparison with the market. This is probably not as important, but it may help us drive the implementation of results. It will be easier for us to use the analytics outputs in industries where this is seen as the standard, for example, the use of client scoring for debt. In other words, if we are followers, meaning many companies in the same industry have already been running these types of analytics, it may be easier to leverage the analytics outputs of a project. On the other hand, it may be more difficult for leaders.

TRY TO ANSWER THE FOLLOWING QUESTIONS:
- [ ] *Can you describe KPIs (metrics) that you monitor regularly?*
- [ ] *Are the KPIs (metrics) generated automatically?*
- [ ] *Is a description of the KPIs (metrics) available?*
- [ ] *Do you have any automatized prediction models?*
- [ ] *Do you have data available for any type of analysis you would like to run?*
- [ ] *Do you have integrated data?*
- [ ] *Can you show us a list of products/regions/… with descriptions? Does everyone in your department use this list? Is this list used companywide?*
- [ ] *Does your company have a data warehouse or any analytical database?*

1.1.4   Combination of factors

In the end, we need to summarize all the aspects mentioned above together and combine analytics maturity, stakeholder maturity, and company maturity. This is visualised in Figure 1.4.

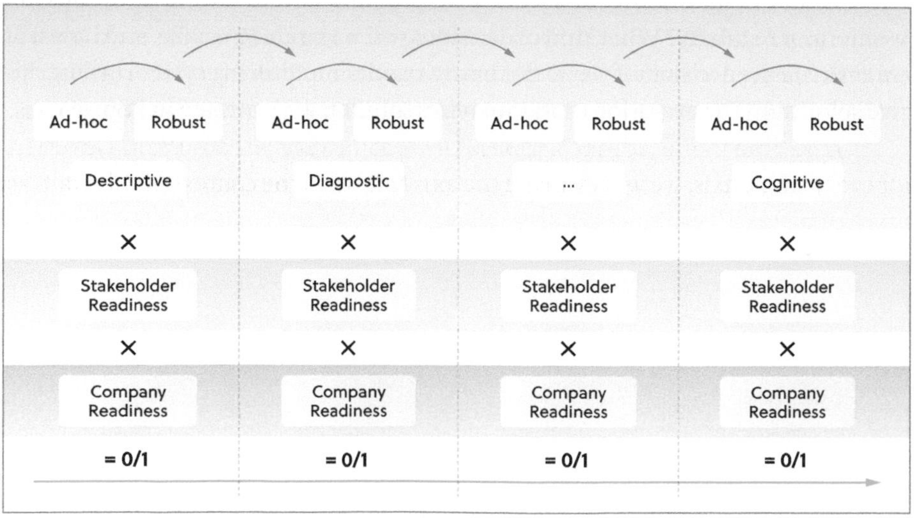

Figure 1.4: Holistic overview of analytics maturity factors

What we really want is the combination of all three together, and none should be missing. As we move more to the right, it becomes more important that the stakeholders and the company buy in. Still, analytics maturity could be depicted as a line. It is difficult to skip any step, and stakeholder (company) maturity is likely to decrease with the complexity of the analytics solution (Descriptive → Predictive).

As you can see, the results are not black and white. However, thinking about analytics maturity from various perspectives will help us understand what analytical work is needed and lead (or at least influence) a discussion with stakeholders.

Analytics maturity determines the direction of every analytics project. Based on the company's agility, this direction can still be modified later, but we know, or we should know, what goals we want to achieve and what the purpose (business value) of the project is.

We cannot jump onto a higher level of analytics maturity without specific experiences from the lower levels and concrete ideas supported by at least some experience or recommendations from the level of analytics maturity we want to achieve. Unless, of course, we are pioneers discovering completely new procedures and techniques.

1.1.5   Connection with the type of analytics and time frame

It is essential to realize that at this point, we have made two important steps in the project evaluation, although both are hidden in analytics maturity. First, we have evaluated the type of analytics: is it descriptive, diagnostic, predictive, or cognitive? Second, we have looked at the project's time frame – is it more ad-hoc or robust? Based on the type of analytics (we can even call this a prerequisite for any further project categorization), we can look at analytics maturity, measured considering the analytics landscape, stakeholder maturity, and company maturity. Keep these two considerations (the type of analytics and the time frame) in mind when you are reading the next axis as well. They are the most important inputs for the categorization process.

The time frame (ad-hoc x robust), especially, may be confusing. However, for every single axis, we will evaluate the axis feature in the context of this trait, as well as the type of analytics – but that is a more understandable trait. Within analytics maturity, the project's time frame can influence how we do the analytical work itself, which is different from how we can do it. Let us look at two examples (both for ad-hoc projects) that may make this easier to understand.

Descriptive ad-hoc project

A descriptive analytics project may be done by drawing a picture (a chart) and pasting it into a presentation. Or it could be done by asking for a data set over an email, storing a text file on the local computer and integrating data in an Excel manual.

Another user could go further and prepare a set of automation rules (in such a case, macros) that will help to repeat a task if needed. Even a more experienced user could use a personal database (run and stored on a local computer as well). When talking about the most mature environment (company), an ad-hoc analytical ecosystem may already be ready for such cases. This could be running on the cloud, provided as a standard service in the company – but still fully dedicated to ad-hoc tasks.

Predictive ad-hoc project

We can conduct an ad-hoc analysis on our computer without following any coding standards, even when we have an advanced self-service analytics environment at our disposal. Again, this might be a good choice because it might take less time. Alternatively, the user could choose a completely opposite approach and comply with existing standards from the beginning – despite the fact that they are aware of the ad-hoc character of work.

Remember:

We will spend a lot of time describing this issue in more detail in the following chapters. However, it is important to realize that analytical work, both ad-hoc and robust, can be done using various means. This is very visible for robust projects, but the same is true for ad-hoc analytical projects (despite the fact that we are not expecting it for the ad-hoc type of work). To put it simply, the fact that we are working on an ad-hoc analytics project does not necessarily mean it will be done purely manually; there may also be significant differences in the delivery.

To conclude this chapter, let us have a look at Figure 1.5. Stakeholder maturity and company analytics maturity play a significant role in our projects from an analytics maturity point of view. Defining the project goals, understanding the journey needed for delivery, stepping out from the project silo if the project is meant to be integrated with other processes or other company systems – all this must be considered and seen as equally important for both an ad-hoc or a robust project. The analytics landscape and market are key factors for robust projects, but in ad-hoc projects, they do not represent significant factors, limitations, or risks if they are not assigned particular importance. Of course, this is only true until an ad-hoc project is industrialized into a robust one.

Once we have a concrete idea of the analytics scope, we can review how the company's data may support us through data maturity. Analytics maturity helps us understand what kind of data we need to have – both in terms of content and robustness. Therefore, we will build on this knowledge and look at the project from a data perspective in the following chapter (1.2 Axis 2: Data Maturity).

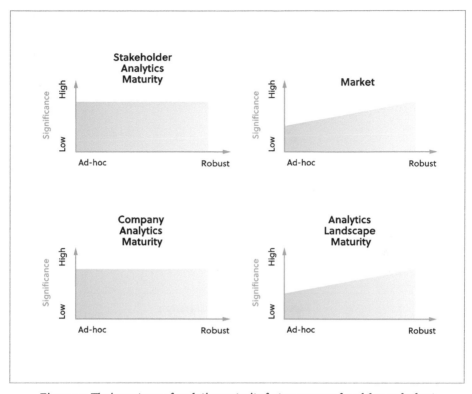

Figure 1.5: The importance of analytics maturity factors can vary for ad-hoc and robust

1.2 Axis 2: Data Maturity

Whereas analytics maturity mainly touches the analytics landscape's complexity, data maturity is all about data itself. As in the previous chapter (1.1 Axis 1: Analytics Maturity), we will try to look at data maturity from many different perspectives to show its complexity. As mentioned before, we should leverage the knowledge gained in the previous chapter. We should already have an idea of which data will be needed (so we can limit the source system that we need to analyse) and understand the robustness of the solution (so we can define how to access the data correctly). In any case, let us have a more in-depth look.

In our experience, discussions on data maturity are often underestimated. Regardless of the analytics maturity and availability of IT solutions and processes, there is no data analytics project without data. The business value of analytics projects lies in the data – making them available, integrating them, or enriching them (e.g., using advanced analytics methods). Therefore, having a stakeholder discussion on the availability and understanding of the data should have the appropriate attention. You also can see it in the flow – we are discussing data maturity before even touching the IT landscape.

We have structured data maturity into four areas (Figure 1.6) and will elaborate on each of them.

Figure 1.6: Data Maturity factors

1.2.1   Are data available?

Data are a core element for every analytics project. These are the data we want to see from a historical or current perspective of what happened or is happening in our organization (e.g., how much money our company earned or is earning right now) or what we can expect will happen in future (how much money our company will probably make). So, for all our analytics questions, we need data that are somehow created, managed, stored, and simply somehow available.

In some specific cases, we can start to work without full access to the data. From the data perspective, this could mean that data are available only partly (dummy data) or not at all. This approach can only be used for prototyping or experimentation and only for specific tasks (defining calculations, performance trials, show visualisation...). In any case, the task should not depend on the data content itself but more on data structures or data volume. "Dummy" data may help us speed up a project at the beginning (or at the beginning of a specific phase), so it could be helpful in cases when we have to make a significant effort to address data availability. Nevertheless, sooner or later, we will need real and fair data.

Speaking of data availability in the context of analytics project failures and their data maturity view, we can split data availability into the following groups describing where data are available, how they are available from a technical point of view, and how data are (can be) used. Typically, we have data, but can we use them? We have data, and we can use them, but how can we use them? Are there any constraints we need to consider?

Data origin (what kind/type of data) = where data are available

Every company has data. There is a great deal of data rolling around everywhere. If the company invests in data integration and centralization and prepares one central storage, most of the data will probably be available promptly, covering the first part of data availability. At least descriptive data like dimensions and code tables and data on sales or orders might exist in one place. In this case, we need nothing but to seek new data required by our needs. However, a situation like this is rare. Depending on the company size and maturity, there can be many different systems, different processes on how data are used, and different places where data are stored. Seeking the right data is a very demanding and risky process, and more so if we work with data from different sources and integrate them.

Aside from company data, we have data that are prepared and managed externally, outside of the company. This is a trend of the last few years, and these data are called public or open data. These data should not be critical for our project. If they are, we need to pay extra attention to why we need precisely this data and check that there is no other way to produce the same data or the same information quality at our company. Likely, a similar or the same data set is already available at the company, for a different project, for instance, so instead of inviting redundant integration, we can review and possibly supplement an existing data feed with the needs of our project. It is essential to pay attention to how credible the given data source and data source owner is, what connection and description are available, and what conditions for its usage exist. We should also have a backup plan if data sources become unavailable, depending on whether our project is ad-hoc or long-term. Once we have downloaded or integrated this data into some process, they will probably need to be integrated with company data, requiring additional effort if direct integration is missing.

Once we know what data we need (internal or external), someone must answer whether we can use this data. There can be compliance, security, regulatory, or political limitations that can prevent us from using them, force us to discover another way, redesign our solution and architecture, or cause a failure. We will dive deeper into security concerns in a later chapter (1.2.4 Is data security considered?).

Technical availability (how we can connect) = how data are available from a technical point of view

All data must be stored somehow. As in the case of the data itself, we can be satisfied with data provided as extracts by flat files in some parts of our analytics project. This is a compelling approach for ad-hoc projects: doing experiments and working on the very first iterations with stakeholders, especially if getting data in other technical ways is complicated and there is no clear understanding of the final solution design or if the data are prepared as part of the project itself (data integration as part of the project).

However, in most cases, when a central data solution is not built (or does not contain all the data we need), data are stored in an underlying transactional database of the source system. Only some source systems have analytics storage available as well – in which data are available for consumption by other applications. In any case, there may be a strict technical limitation on how we are authorized to connect (for example, we can connect only during the non-peak period of the source system, or we need to wait till data processing is finished). Additionally, we need to understand whether we can identify the data in the source system and understand the complexity of the data structures provided. It could mean that only some data are available to load, despite more data being stored in the system itself. If we need to combine data from more source systems, we will probably need a place to perform data integration (technically, it could be solved in many ways).

There is also a new trend, which has become popular in recent years – it is called API. Many systems are built to accommodate communication over the internet or intranet using modern protocols for internal system communication. We can imagine a combination of RDMS data with data from the IoT on a real-time basis. If API is available, we need to consider the maturity of the analytics tools and platforms we use and our way of working with data. For example, an approach that is not good is to load a few MBs or even GBs of data using API.

Once we have identified the source of our data (internal, external, database, or API), we need to start addressing connectivity with two main questions:

1.   Is it possible to connect the data in data source XYZ?
2.   How can we connect the XYZ data source?

For a) there is probably a simple yes or no answer, or yes with a condition – in most cases, conditions are set by the security or compliance perspective more than the technical. If I cannot connect data due to technical issues, then there may be a different way, impacting our analytics project architecture or delivery to a greater or lesser degree. For an ad-hoc project, we can continue without any solution. We can simply ask the data steward and get the requested data this way. Unfortunately, no robust project can operate while relying on this manual way unless we want to invest extra effort (and costs) or have a good reason for it – forecasting preliminary data, for instance.

In the case of b), the answer is not as straightforward as for a). The technical problem will not be as prevalent; we have various options for connecting to data, but a few will cause us real challenges. A situation that will not pose a challenge will be when we have the drivers and connection string with all the necessary authentication in place and approval from the data steward/owner to use this data. At the opposite end of the scale, we have a situation in which we are connecting a new data source with no experience on the project or the data source side because it has not been done before. We are positioned somewhere in between for most analytics projects, which applies to every type – flat file, database, or API. We must always expect something to break, especially if our company ecosystem is extensive and contains many independent components.

Technical availability may play an additional role for specific, scientific, and advanced analytics projects. Plotting thousands of points into a map, clustering information together or calculating a vast formula on the fly will create higher demands, not only for the visualization components but also for data availability. Using specific data sources like graph databases and vertical or in-memory data storage can significantly affect our analytics project's resources, costs, time, and requirements and make it more prone to potential failure.

Data usability or data readiness (how we use data) = how data are (can be) used

Ad-hoc data exports are good enough for the initial phases of analytics projects, prototyping, and situations in which the requirements allow that. However, no matter who exported it, it must meet the possible limitations described above. A typical example can be a one-time advance analytics project, e.g., a finance simulation. Additionally, a few runs in a year can be fine, but doing the same ad-hoc data export again may become inefficient if we want to run the same advanced analytics finance simulation every month or repeat it weekly. In this case, automation becomes the better choice. The automation format depends on several factors like integration with other data sources or the requirements for data freshness. With automation and data freshness, we come to the next topic – Service Level Agreement. This clearly plays a more significant role in more complex and reusable solutions and brings more complexity to analytics projects.

As soon as we start addressing an automation problem, we can tackle specific issues. For example, we need to understand whether the data will be loaded in full extracts (so each time we will be loading data, we will take the full data set) or deltas will be available (so we will only be downloading the changes in data). Understanding the data set's specifics is crucial for project planning (as different approaches have different complexity, advantages, and problems).

Now we have data, we know how to connect them, and we can use these data, but there is still another potential problem that can cause our analytics project to fail or at least stumble – data quality. We might make a significant effort on getting quality data for our projects, especially if we are building a complex solution. Data from various systems can be wholly different; there might not be specific keys, or the reference integrity may not exist at all. We can also integrate a system based on totally different principles of storing data (RDMS and document database system, OLAP…) where extra attention must be paid specifically to long term solutions.

■ **TRY TO ANSWER THE FOLLOWING QUESTIONS:**
☐ *Do you know where data are stored physically?*
☐ *Do you know how to access them?*
☐ *Do you know the granularity of the data?*
☐ *Has someone already used the required data set for analysis?*
☐ *Do you know the team that is managing the source system?*
☐ *Do you know the data formats?*
☐ *Do you know how often the data are updated?*
☐ *Is data provided using any service, e.g., Data as a Service or API?*
☐ *Is there any agreement or contract with the data source provided on the data provisioning?*

1.2.2 Are data integrated?

Using one data set might not be enough, or our data set may not contain all the needed information. For instance, we can compare data from IoT streams with finance data stored in the company's SAP to compare or predict our finance impact based on real data coming from the company's manufacturing division, so management can promptly react to all anomalies that might occur. In such a case, we benefit from pre- built integration on the company or division level.

Let us take a quick look at the concept (logical flow) of data processing. We can distinguish between different stages of data – all of them have a different feature (quality). As a key definition, we know source, raw, derived, and integrated data – these concepts and relationships are visualized in Figure 1.7.

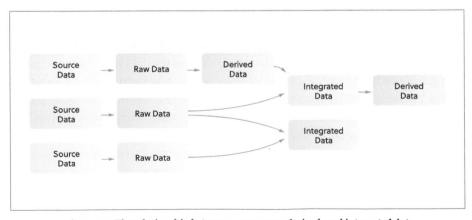

Figure 1.7: The relationship between source, raw, derived, and integrated data

Source data are stored in the source systems (transactional ones). If we want to leverage them, we need access to the source system directly, which could be problematic for many reasons. One of them is the performance of the source system itself – it is not usually designed for analytical tasks. So, if you run a complex query against the transactional system, the system itself may encounter performance issues (as it is designed for transactional tasks, but not for analytical ones). That is why the data from the source system is usually moved to new data storage for analytical purposes.

Raw data are usually a plain copy of source data, merely moved to an analytics data storage. Only technical data transformation is usually applied. For example, we can change the data format, the data type of the columns, or apply technical data quality rules. Within this data move, no business focus transformation will occur.

Derived data include a business transformation. It means that additional business value is generated during the creation of the derived data set. That could be done in many ways and at different stages of the data flow (as you can see in Figure 1.7, we have two different blocks representing the derived data set). The first one (on the left) represents derived data created directly from the raw data set. It could refer to any business cleaning of data that needs to happen to render data more understandable. It could include transformation, like selecting/combining the relevant columns (which represent the product's name) or deriving a new calculated column based on one raw data product. In any case, the additional business value is not generated by integrating data from more raw data products. The second one (following integrated data) is designed to make integrated data more consumable. Once again, it could choose the right column for the product name from the integrated data set. Any derived data product could be used as a "source" for additional data flows. That means it could potentially be used as an input for other integrated data product creation.

Integrated data is the middle piece, which combines data from multiple data sources (raw data products). This includes all transformations that need to happen to make two different data sets comparable and understandable. It might look like an easy task, but challenges like different granularity, different code tables, or different approaches to time dimensions need to be dealt with. That may require many tables and transformations that may be difficult to read and understand, which is why a derived data set can be created from an integrated data set.

The approach described above is only conceptual. It means that raw data is not necessarily just one table. It could be a set of tables with the same characteristics. For example, exporting all data (tables) from one source system could still be described as raw data. Sometimes, we can also use the "product" concept. If we want to have data as a product, we need to add additional services around the data. For example, we need to have someone who owns the data, who can grant access to them, who ensures the data quality within the data set... We simply need to have a product owner defining and providing additional services around the data product.

The best situation for an analytics project is when an integrated data product exists. This could bring described data, which can be used as the foundation for our analytics project.

If a company invests in a centralized data warehouse, some of the required data will likely be integrated. Moreover, integration can be extended to more objectives like data quality or data description (mentioned later in this chapter), and our project can just focus on delivering the missing pieces needed for the solution delivery. Data integration touches on data availability regarding the necessary connections or the challenges we must overcome before data becomes available (connectivity, drivers, approvals).

However, in many cases, especially when introducing new data or processes, we do not have any integration, and we need to decide how the data will be integrated. This will subsequently affect the discussion about technology choices (IT maturity), the resources needed, and the costs/benefits of the data integration.

Unless we use a single data source in the analytics solution, we perform data integration at some point, meaning we integrate data sets (inputs) into integrated data sets (outputs). Integration can happen in many places – e.g., in the data warehouse, in the data science algorithms, or the reporting tools; anywhere there is a good reason for it. If we know that data are only needed for data science algorithms, it does not make sense to invest any effort for integration into the data warehouse. The more complex the project is, the more data integration we need to consider.

Since data can be stored everywhere, data integration is a failure risk if we talk about data structures or formats. In our example at the beginning of this chapter, we use data from totally different architectures, and we can expect different data formats – the JSON format for IoT versus the complex relation table structure in SAP. Today, data are not only stored in relational databases, but when thinking of various multi-dimensional structures, document databases, big data landscapes, or more or less large files, we are dealing with a complex area that brings many risks and potential challenges to analytics projects.

The feasibility of the data integration of two data sets can be limited even if the formats are the same from a technological perspective – e.g., if the data do not contain attributes that could be used for integration. Therefore, we need raw data described to evaluate the data integration. It could be even more complicated – data could have a common attribute, but the definition of attributes could differ. Alternatively, the definition might be the same but unfortunately created by two different people, which could lead to misunderstanding. That is usually easily overcome within ad-hoc projects, but in robust projects, integration needs to function smoothly in every single situation (every single combination of both data sets on the source). Sometimes, describing this logic is impossible as it differs based on the given business situation. In such a case, we need to include adequate tools or processes into the analytics solution to ensure this possibility. Not only from a technical perspective (we have an interface in which we can map/correct data) but also from a data processing perspective (how is this manual correction initiated, is there any workflow around, and how the dependencies with other data processing are managed).

A specific situation could be connected to the time dimension challenge. It looks straightforward, but data must be aligned from a time perspective as well. Furthermore, even though two data sources could be described well and appear to be easy to integrate, this different approach to time may pose a significant challenge. For example, one source system could allow retrospective data changes by updating a value (in history). Another could do the same over a new "transaction" that changes the history result (but both are available). Alternatively, some systems could send the monthly data immediately after the end of the month, and another one may need a couple of days for data processing. These discrepancies can have a significant impact on the complexity of implementation and data integration.

The creation of an integrated data set could be a separate project of its own. Alternatively, it may be hidden, and creating an integrated data set is a key pre-condition for delivering analytics results. As such, the project may be similar to delivering a report, but 80% of the work will need to be related to the data integration landscape. We will be discussing this in more depth in the WoW chapter (3.2 Ways of working - WoW).

TRY TO ANSWER THE FOLLOWING QUESTIONS:
- [ ] *Has anyone used the data before with some other data set?*
- [ ] *Do you know the definition of dimensions across the data sources?*
- [ ] *Are you sure that the data format in the two source systems is the same?*
- [ ] *Are you sure that the granularity of data in the two source systems is the same?*
- [ ] *Do you know how the source systems tackle the time dimension?*
- [ ] *Is any DWH solution in place?*
- [ ] *What is the company strategy for integrated data?*
- [ ] *What is the delivery model for DWH? Is there a central team in place?*
- [ ] *Is the integrated data a valuable result of analytics projects in general?*

1.2.3   Are data described?

While data availability tells us whether we can technically use the data for the project, data description (or metadata) tells us how easily we can understand the data we need to address the analytics problem. It is essential to acknowledge that getting technical access to the data is not enough; understanding them is just as important. A lack of data comprehension leads to longer implementation times or data quality issues in the solution.

Documenting data or metadata is a significant element of larger data governance concepts. The purpose of this publication is not to discuss data governance in full but to focus on the elements that we believe are key for framing analytics projects. When setting up a new analytics project, it is crucial to take the current company data governance model and services into account and understand the opportunities (e.g., does the company have business glossaries or data dictionaries I can reuse for my assignment?) as well as constraints (e.g., what are the practices or processes for documenting the metadata for newly acquired data sources?).

The need to document the data varies considerably based on the project type, and connections to other axes also play a significant role here. For example, the approach for a project combining three new data sources with the outlook for reusability by multiple consumers will likely generate more metadata management work than an ad-hoc advanced analysis performed on a well-known top data set, and we should manage the stakeholders' expectations accordingly.

Speaking of describing and understanding data for analytics project delivery, we structure the area as follows:

1. Types of metadata: business, technical, operational
2. Types of data sets in terms of the level of integration: raw, derived, integrated

Business, technical, and operational metadata need to be evaluated

For the purposes of this book, we shall consider three types of metadata: business, technical and operational metadata, and each of them will matter in different types of assignments.

Business metadata (e.g., the business meaning of a given attribute) will be needed almost for any project (though not for all the people participating in the project) as analysts will need a business understanding of the data used for data integrations or analytical calculations. The need for a higher level of governance will increase with the number of metadata, the number of consumers and more robust projects. What if the business description of the data is not available yet? Acquiring this information needs to be planned for, and we need to ensure the cooperation of the subject matter expert (likely the data steward).

Technical metadata (e.g., what is the data type of the column?) and operational metadata (e.g., when was the data set refreshed for the last time?) will typically play a more prominent role in robust projects rather than ad-hoc ones.

There is a clear relationship to IT maturity as we need to understand the technology, processes, and practices available and used for the metadata management in the company in order to discuss the feasibility and estimates on the governance of such metadata.

A description of raw data does not imply a description of integrated data

The above chapter (1.2.1 Are data available?) on data availability highlighted that it is vital to distinguish raw vs integrated (vs derived) data sets. People may think that when two data sources are well-described, they automatically contain a description of the integrated data set. In many cases, this is quite far from reality and causes misleading expectations for multiple reasons (examples, a non-exhaustive list):

— Input data sets may have different granularity, and the granularity of the output data set is unclear – e.g., we integrate actual sales every month with forecasted sales every quarter.
— A mismatch of attributes – e.g., both data sets have an attribute account, but it means something very different in each of them.
— Different hierarchies/code lists in each data set – e.g., we report on the sales of car components and integrate data sets from multiple markets but are the components the same across the markets?
— Different descriptions details – e.g., the description in one of the data sets is missing a detail needed to describe an attribute.
— Two data sets have different historization patterns.

Therefore, it is essential to determine whether integrated data (if needed) are described and, if not, reflect this in the project scope.

TRY TO ANSWER THE FOLLOWING QUESTIONS:

☐ *Is there a central solution for describing analytics artefacts (report, KPI, tables…) within the company?*
☐ *Do you know the standard definition of metrics used in the department/company?*
☐ *Does the source system include a described interface for data consumption?*
☐ *Has the source system ever provided data sets to someone else?*
☐ *Do you have a contact for the "data owner"?*
☐ *Does the "data owner" or "data steward" role even exist in the company?*
☐ *Is there a guideline that describes the approach to metadata? Is it for technical, operational, or business metadata?*
☐ *Does the export of the data include any log files?*
☐ *Do you know how often data are updated?*
☐ *How quick or straightforward is it to get or find an answer regarding the business meaning of the data?*
☐ *Are there data models in place? (conceptual, logical, physical)*
☐ *Do you have access to the documentation of business and technological transformations in existing data pipelines relevant to your project?*

1.2.4   Is data security considered?

Data security is the last aspect of data maturity. As already mentioned, we need to understand whether we can use data (or, more precisely, how we can use data).

In general, data security may surprisingly be a business problem. Data security is about the restriction on how to use data. There could be many reasons why we are not authorized to work with the data as we wish. Let us name a few:

—   The first may be connected to the company strategy. For example, will we allow the sales results of one region to be shown in another region? Do we even show detailed transactions (every single deal)? Will we show aggregated numbers only (overall sales for all products)? Are these restrictions valid for all the metrics, or we will implement the restriction only on some of them (for example, we can show the plans, but not the actuals)? What restrictions will be implemented across the products we are managing? We need to know the answers to all these questions to understand whether we can deliver the analysis or even actually use the analysis result.

—   The second may lie in regulation – we cannot see specific data about the customer. It may be the personal identification number, credit card number, or address. Simply, regulation dictates what we can and cannot show. This problem becomes more complex when we want to use data from different countries. In such a case, we need to understand the regulation on both sides and potentially integrate the data to comply with the strictest regulation.

—   Another reason could be licensing. For example, the company buys country data from an external vendor on the local level within the market, and according to the license agreement, the data can be accessed only by users within the specific market and not globally. This may become even more complex when specific attributes of the data sets are meant for global use while others must remain local.

—   The last complication could be caused by the fact that some data cannot even leave the country (region). We are not authorized to physically store them outside of the country (which is an IT problem), but such a situation could influence the analysis approach.

In general, the complexity of business defined data security may become overwhelming. It may be highly time-consuming to find consensus (even within the company), sometimes even impossible, due to different groups within the company. Security and compliance teams will always push for stricter restrictions since they need to approve the solution from a security point of view. On the other hand, the business team will always promote data availability, as the business insight could be important for them. Once again, finding the right balance may be the most important and challenging task. The project may even become impossible to implement, despite the fact, that there is a technical solution for solving security issues. It could relate to the company's risk appetite (once again, you can see the connection to analytics maturity, specifically to the stakeholder/company analytics maturity level). In this context, market maturity could be critical (there are different regulations for different industries in place).

As soon as we understand the business security model, we need to be able to translate it into IT requirements. This may be critical for IT tool selection as some tools do not necessarily implement the required level of security (or the complexity could become challenging). So let us look at some possible descriptions that the IT department could leverage. We tried to order them from the easiest to the most complex, but as we have mentioned, it depends on the IT toolset to a great extent, so please consider this a list of examples regardless of the order (in reality, we may encounter a multiple of these):

— No security – publicly available data
— Security based on NDA (non-disclosure agreement)
— Security on the application level (access is granted to the application, but all data in the application can be consumed in case the access is granted)
— Security on a "high" object level – for example, security managed on the report (folder) level
— Security on a "low" object level – for example, security managed on the object in the report (file in the folder) level
— Data security managed on the object level (table) – for example, you can see the report, but only some objects are filled with data
— Data security managed on the row level – for example, you can see only the results for your department
— Data security with differences on the granular and aggregated level (you cannot see the granular data like sales transactions, but you can see aggregated results like the summary of the transaction)
— Data security on the row and column level – different security needs to be implemented for different combinations of rows and columns (transaction and metrics within the transaction). For example, you can see the number of transactions but not the volume.
— Anonymization of data (to remove sensitive data) is needed.

Additionally, different security modes may be needed for different roles (user groups). Security restrictions for developers/admins of the system pose an intriguing problem. These people typically need to see production data as they need to be able to track any data transformation happening within the system. Additionally, developers can hardly create a predictive model when they do not see very granular data.

As was already mentioned, finding a balance between restrictions and the possibility to gain insights is crucial and could influence the project's final success. We can end up in a situation in which the number of consumers we have is very limited because either we do not grant them access to the tool, or we do, but the content is not interesting for them because it is overly aggregated or anonymized. We have already mentioned that the project should generate value over the additional insight generated. If we limit the audience/consumers significantly, we are also limiting the reach of insight, which means that we are decreasing the rentability of the project. If you think about it, we might not even be able to start a project due to the restrictions on data, regardless of the benefits that could be generated from the additional insight.

At the end of this chapter, let us have a look at a simple visualisation:

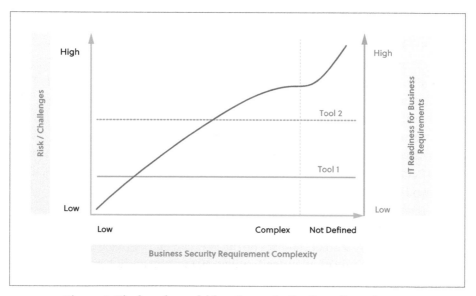

Figure 1.8: The dependency of risk on the complexity of security requirements

In Figure 1.8, you can see the relation between the risk/potential challenges on the project and the complexity of the business security definition. In any case, the highest risk comes from "undefined requirements". In such a case, we do not know what we should prepare for, meaning any estimate may be wrong (from the perspective of finance, time, and the number of consumers). Additionally, the selection of the IT landscape may be completely wrong, which could require a complete technical redesign later.

TRY TO ANSWER THE FOLLOWING QUESTIONS:
- [ ] *Is there a security model that is described in general?*
- [ ] *Is there a security model that is described for concrete data sets?*
- [ ] *Can I use the data set? What are the restrictions?*
- [ ] *Can I share the data set? What are the restrictions?*
- [ ] *At which level of granularity would you like to share the data?*
- [ ] *Will any sensitive data (personal ID, credit card....) be available for the end-users?*
- [ ] *Will there be any sensitive data in the data sources?*
- [ ] *Has anyone used the same data before? Was this data shared across the company?*
- [ ] *Do the data move across regions?*
- [ ] *Does the company have GDPR guidance?*
- [ ] *Has there been a similar project that implemented similar security restrictions during the implementation?*
- [ ] *Is the security requirement a standard part of IT guidelines?*
- [ ] *Does my data/report storage comply with security standards?*
- [ ] *What do I need to comply with security standards?*

1.2.5   Connection with the type of analytics and time frame

As in the previous chapter (1.1 Axis 1: Analytics Maturity), let us connect this axis with the type of analytics and "time frame". When we consider and evaluate data maturity, we need to keep both these assumptions in mind. There could be different requirements for data maturity and different approaches to solving the problem and evaluating the data readiness. We can demonstrate this with the following examples (ad-hoc projects).

Data security

Data security can easily be addressed with an NDA for an ad-hoc project when we are sure detailed data will not be presented (there will be no drill down possibility). As such, the only one who can see the detailed data (regardless of whether it is customer individual region detail) is just a developer. Or, conversely, we can easily limit the target audience to the top management – they are authorized to see any details available.

Access to data

For an ad-hoc project, we can export data from existing reports – meaning from existing visualization. Therefore, instead of using the direct connection to the underlying database tables or views (used by the report), we will simply export data from the report object directly.

Once again, the evaluation of data maturity for a specific project depends mainly on the defined project assumptions and the type of analytics, which also plays an important role. As you can see in Figure 1.9, data are equally crucial for every analytics project (ad-hoc or robust). However, security considerations may not be as important to consider for ad-hoc projects. Rather than on security, we will focus on data integration or data description, which varies according to the analytics project type. For ad-hoc projects, we do not need to consider data integration, but it can help us make our lives easier, assuming data are described in some way.

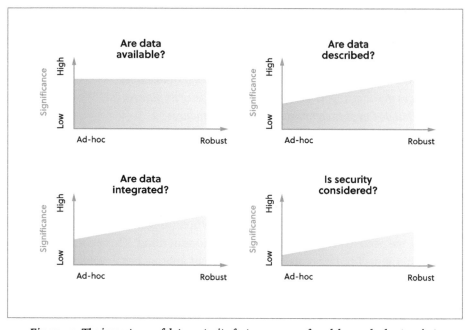

Figure 1.9: The importance of data maturity factors can vary for ad-hoc and robust projects

Now, we can move to the last axis description. As we know what analytics problem we must address and understand the data landscape from both the business and the technical perspective (including security), we can jump to selecting IT tools. We should have much better clarity regarding which tools may be needed, and we can evaluate whether such a tool is available within the company.

1.3   Axis 3: IT Maturity

In general, IT maturity (also referred to as the IT landscape) focuses on the readiness of the tools and technical processes to implement data analytics projects. Different toolsets are needed for different project types, and the availability and maturity of tools are crucial for the successful delivery of the project. If IT maturity is not suffi-cient, implementing a data analytics project could quickly change into an IT project with a focus on the performance of the tools and the processes around them (espe-cially for robust projects). Alternatively, selecting the wrong tool at the beginning of the project (typically an ad-hoc project) may lead to a complex reimplementa-tion during the industrialization phase (changing the project from ad-hoc into the robust or project integration into the solution).

We choose the same approach as for analytics and data maturity, and we split the IT landscape into several areas (Figure 1.10).

Answering these questions should give us sufficient clarity to limit the risk and help us initiate the right conversation with stakeholders.

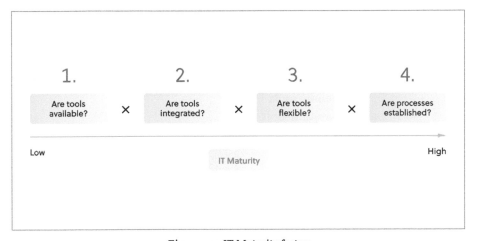

Figure 1.10: IT Maturity factors

In general, this is highly connected with enterprise architecture (especially with data analytics architecture, but not only that), which is defined for the company. Therefore, we will simplify our point of view and express an assumption that the architecture is equal to the IT landscape. Let us have a look at every single question separately.

1.3.1 Are the tools available?

Many tools may be needed for the data analytics project implementation. Differ-ent toolsets may be required depending on the analytics problem definition both in terms of the analytics type (descriptive, prescriptive) and the time frame (ad-hoc/robust). Therefore, the best approach may be to identify the analytical capability needed at the beginning of the project and map it onto the available tools. One possi-ble way to do so is to have a look at the data journey:

1.   Acquire data (ad-hoc/robust)
2.   Integrate and transform data (ad-hoc/robust)
3.   Generate insight from data (ad-hoc/robust)
     —   Visualize data (ad-hoc/robust)
     —   Create an advanced analytics (AA) model
         of the data (ad-hoc/robust)
     —   Visualize data (including) results of AA models (ad-hoc/robust)

The previous step (evaluation of data and analytics maturity) should already give us insight into what steps will be needed and whether we are doing an ad-hoc or robust project. We shall now move one level deeper and have a look at some tools that could be needed (the list is by no means comprehensive):

1.   Acquire data (ad-hoc/robust)
     —   Data exchange tools (loading data from the external environment)
     —   Data storage for acquired data
2.   Integrate and transform data (ad-hoc/robust)
     —   Data modelling tools
     —   Data preparation tools
     —   ETL tools
     —   ELT tools
     —   Scripting tools
     —   Data storage for integrated data sets
3.   Generate insight from data (ad-hoc/robust)
     —   Visualize data (ad-hoc/robust)
         —   Reporting tools
         —   Custom visualization tool
     —   Create an AA model of the data (ad-hoc/robust)
         —   AA modelling environment
         —   AA model deployment environment
         —   AA model transactional storage
         —   AA model result storage
         —   AA model monitoring
     —   Visualize the results of AA models (ad-hoc/robust)
         —   Visualization of AA results only in AA tools
         —   Visualizations of the AA model inte-
             grated with other visualizations

As soon as we understand what steps need to happen on our (project) analytics journey, we can look at the concrete tools that should be required. One tool may easily be used for multiple steps, and some could be required only for robust projects. We also need to understand what a tool being available means.

The definition may differ from the license point of view and the tool capability point of view. We need to clearly understand what tasks will be undertaken in which tool and ensure that the selected technology meets the key requirements. If we identify the top requirements soon enough (examples – write back on top of reporting, embedding analytical insights into other pages), we can shape the solution's architecture or manage expectations correctly.

Sometimes the discussion is not only about the tool as such but also about the best practices within the company (we will discuss processes later). For example, Excel is currently quite a powerful tool that can be used for almost everything in the analytical area – you can do data integration, data preparation, data visualization, and even AA model construction when you have the right person and the right IT landscape to do so.

The definition of tools and the tasks that will be completed in each tool helps us identify the right people that we need to include in the project because it describes the technology requirements. Sometimes, it could also be the other way around – the available skillset could define the toolset. Especially with emerging technologies, we can find a great technology fit but not sufficient resource coverage. In any case, let us assume that if the company has a tool, there are resources as well.

TRY TO ANSWER THE FOLLOWING QUESTIONS:
- [ ] *What tool do we have for (data preparation, data modelling…)?*
- [ ] *What is the license model for the tool?*
- [ ] *Is there any limitation on how to use the existing toolset?*
- [ ] *What toolset was used by the last similar analytics project and why?*
- [ ] *Do the standard tools cover every analytical step?*
- [ ] *Are the tools scalable enough in the case that the project will bring a significant additional performance demand?*
- [ ] *Is the tool stable enough (LTS vs Beta, education edition vs enterprise)?*
- [ ] *Is a tool knowledge base available?*
- [ ] *Is any particular experience needed to start using the tool?*
- [ ] *Is it an on-premise or cloud solution?*
- [ ] *Is the tool provided as PaaS or SaaS?*

1.3.2   Are tools integrated?

The tools availability discussion could quickly turn into many streams, each focusing on different steps needed for the data project. That could be caused for many reasons, the most common being that different teams are responsible for different components of the solution. However, we still need to keep in mind that at the end of the day, we need to have a toolset that works together.

Tools have many overlaps and technical/functional limitations. The vendors' strategy is to cover maximum functionality within one tool. We have already discussed an Excel example, but the same is valid for many tools. That may cause tension between different teams about which tool should be used for which step (as there are more options). Using one tool for multiple steps ensures better integration, but on the other hand, one universal tool usually has a limitation in concrete tasks. An illustration of such a problem could be a tendency to include AA components into the visualization toolset. We need to decide whether the complexity and flexibility of AA components embedded into the reporting tool are sufficient for our goal or may create a limitation. The problem of tool overlaps is growing – it is also very closely connected with the processes around the tools. A specific task may be possible in the tool, but it does not necessarily have to be supported from the company perspective. Slightly more about this topic is in the chapter 1.3.5 The number of tools paradox.

When we do the evaluation correctly, we should be able to categorize:

1.   Tools are not available.
2.   Tools are available; integration is not possible in the current landscape.
3.   Tools are available; integration is technically possible but not tested.
4.   Tools are available; integration is technically done but not tested.
5.   Tools are available; integration is technically done
        and tested (other solutions already use it).
6.   Tools are available, integration is technically done and tested
        (other solutions already use it), and limitations are well described.
        However, even at this level, there could be many ways the integration
        is done. Currently, the most mature way uses microservices
        defined within every single tool, ensuring smooth cooperation
        and potentially the easy change of any ecosystem component.

Different integration and limitations are crucial for differing types of analytics (see the chapter 1.1 Axis 1: Analytics Maturity). We need to be careful when reusing approaches defined by other projects because we cannot be sure that these projects have the same scope (even though it could be said that both projects should do predictive tasks).

It is critically important to understand the IT landscape for a robust project. In an ad-hoc project, many steps can be done manually, and automation and seamless integration are not necessary prerequisites. Our goal is to deploy robust projects into production, so any missing integration could lead to long discussions about the right integration and processes that need to be established.

TRY TO ANSWER THE FOLLOWING QUESTIONS:
☐ *Were the recommended tools used together on some analytics projects?*
☐ *Are the boundaries between the tools defined? Are there*
best practices on when to use which tool?
☐ *Is there a single security model for all the tools that should be used?*
☐ *Is it possible to access tools outside of the company network?*
☐ *What methods are used for integration? (e.g., API, microservice concept)*

1.3.3   Are the tools flexible?

Toolset flexibility is a specific point of view that could be included in any chapter above. However, we believe that it is worth highlighting. It is really about the flexibility of the tool that should be used for a specific area. We should look at the possibility of scaling up a tool, which may allow us to solve a problem only slightly different to one tackled in another project in the same tool. The easiest way to illustrate it would be an example.

Custom visualization

Some concrete analytics problems need to have a specific visualization available to improve insight consumption significantly. Unfortunately, such specific visualization is not commonly available in the standard reporting toolset (mainly because it is specific, and the consumption rate is not high). That may lead us to decide to use a specific tool (not a general reporting tool), as visualization is one of the critical requirements (and the ease of consumption should be another critical requirement of every project).

A different approach could be to "empower" the standard reporting tool by including additional visualization. It also brings a great deal of complexity into the solution. However, from the overall toolset perspective, this could be a better solution than building a customised interface or using a specific application that likely will not meet other criteria.

Installation of an additional library

Another example could be from an advanced analytics area. Usually, we have a standard set of libraries that we are authorized to use to solve analytics problems. However, are we authorized to install an additional library? If yes, what does it mean for the other users of the platform? Is there any established process for doing so, and are we confident that it is easy?

If we think about it in detail, we will always find that there could be something specific in our project. "Flexibility" basically describes our level of confidence that we will be able to solve highly specific scenarios in a common toolset. This is crucial for customer satisfaction and, therefore, for the project's success.

TRY TO ANSWER THE FOLLOWING QUESTIONS:

- [ ] *Does the tool have varied interfaces (data connectors, support for API)?*
- [ ] *Is the tool just WYSIWYG, or does it enable developers to use coding and customize using scripts and parameters?*
- [ ] *Is the tool based on architecture supporting development swarming?*
- [ ] *Is it possible to add custom components to the tools?*
- [ ] *Is there a list of custom components already added to the ecosystem?*
- [ ] *Is there a central team taking care of the custom component?*
- [ ] *Is there a described process (methodology, standards) of how to do it?*
- [ ] *How difficult is it to add a custom component?*

1.3.4 Are processes established?

As soon as we understand the toolset for the project, we need to look at how we are authorized to use it.

As you look at subcategories, you will find that they are closely connected with how to deliver or deploy the project – which could theoretically be out of our scope as we focus on project categorization. However, we believe that it is essential to understand these concepts before the delivery because there could be significant implications, such as:

- Is the project event possible to deliver?
- How quickly can we deliver?
- What are the high-level costs (with a focus on non-analytical work)? What should be counted in?

We are mentioning this as we believe it is crucial for correct stakeholder management, which must happen at the beginning of the projects.

Once again, let us categorize this topic into the following areas:

1. How to gain access to the tool
2. Best practices and methodologies defined and required
3. Deployment standards
4. Support models
5. Delivery model in general – centralization x federated approach
6. Industrialization process

Let us have a look at all these.

How to get access to the tool

This is quite fundamental – what does it mean to have access to a tool? There could be license constraints (which could bring additional costs to the project) and time constraints. Many tools have a very complex licensing mode, and there could be different licensing models (even for different components of the same tool). Sometimes, only basic features are available, but we need to pay additional costs for more advanced components. Occasionally, we can be limited by performance, and other components may be required to scale up. Time constraints are really about the time needed before a developer can start to work on the project. It could be related to the processes of requesting access or the time necessary for installation. However, it could also be about the mandatory training that the developer needs to pass before they get access to the tool (whether it is technical or compliance training). This is important, especially at the beginning of the project, but it could be crucial specifically for quick ad-hoc projects as well. These usually have aggressive timelines and run purely in an agile manner. A couple of the first sprints may easily not be about the burnout of business stories but access processing. To increase the complexity, note that the same problem could materialize when discussing access to data. It may take some time to gain access to the data as such (for the same reasons as mentioned for the toolset).

Best practices and methodologies defined and required

The second question could be more misleading. The existence of best practices and methodologies is commonly understood as a benefit – and that may be true. The existence of "shared experience storage" in any form could help with tackling the problem – regardless of whether it is a technical problem (how to set up technical access to the data set) or an analytics problem (how to conduct a time series analysis in R Studio). On the other hand, "best practices" could be another word for limitations or additional requirements that need to be followed. Additionally, some methodologies may be overly complex for defined tasks, but they can be challenging to change (especially when the project is the first one in a specific area). Below you can find a couple of examples.

How to write a code/develop

Standards around the code (or any other development best practices) are no doubt necessary. However, we need to realize that there could be company best practices/ standards that are not common on the market (for many reasons). Learning them may require a team (initially) and following up on them could mean more extended development. However, it may be necessary from the company standard perspective, and it could be a condition for deployment into production.

Documentation

Documentation is needed and should be part of the development. However, sometimes documentation is very extensive and time-consuming. Sometimes, parts of the documentation require specific software. For example, you may need a database model to deploy a database schematic into the production. For this, you need to have access to a database modelling tool, you need to have someone who can work with the tool, and you need to work in a way that allows the database model to be developed.

Toolset limitations due to specific company implementation

You can have experience with a tool and expect (based on this experience) that the tool could be used in some way. However, the deployment within the company (division…) may constrict some functionality from the process or methodology points of view. Again, this could be well hidden behind best practices. For example, there can be restrictions on modelling the data in a reporting tool due to the performance challenges (which is relevant). Alternatively, you can also face significant overhead for simply updating the script file as your permissions are not sufficient to perform this action, and you need to use a regular company service request and involve more people. This is very connected with the tool overlaps discussed before.

Deployment standards

The third area could also significantly influence the project. We have already discussed documentation (as a must-have condition for deployment), but there could also be impacts on the timing of releases. Some source systems have a regular release (the frequency of such a release could be quite long, for example, even a quarter or half of a year). As such, it could take a significant amount of time before you even gain access to the data. The same is valid with project deployment into the production – it needs to be coordinated across every single component of the solution, but different tools could have a different frequency.

Additionally, the deployment process itself can be quite time-consuming as it includes "testing". Therefore, the project (specifically a robust one) will always include tension between the number (frequency) of releases and the time needed for the release. There are concepts for limiting the time needed for the deployment, but we still need to understand the standards within the defined toolset.

Support model

Last but not least is the support model. The support itself is not connected tightly with the project itself, but it could relate to the deployment (the defined support model is a mandatory part of deployment itself). For analytics projects, there are three types of support, in general:

Infrastructure/Tools support

Infrastructure/Tools support is the most basic support that can be provided. It only evaluates/ensures that a service is up and running. That covers areas like server outages, data load failures due to insufficient memory, or the reporting tool being up and running. Usually, this is well established and part of the standard IT operational model.

Data support

The most common problem in data analytics projects is data issues. From a certain perspective, this is a specific situation – all infrastructure is up and running, but the report shows the wrong result (number). In this case, someone who understands data and data flow across the different components of the solution needs to be included. Furthermore, as we are talking about data, such a person needs to have at least a basic business understanding of the data in the system. As you can see, this support is project-specific because it deals with specific data. Standard IT support does not commonly cover this; instead, a specific support team must be established for specific analytics applications.

Analytics model support

Analytics model support goes even further. If an advanced analytics model is in production, we need to monitor the model's performance. If the model has degraded over time, we need a data science expert to validate or update the model. That could mean simple model recalibration, but it could also mean a complex model redesign. Considering that, we need to have the capacity of data scientists dedicated to such an activity.

Delivery model – centralized x federated approach

There could be two different "extremes" in delivery models established for different toolsets. There could be a central delivery team for some capabilities that could help us move ahead; for others, a federated approach could be used.

A centralized approach means there is a team at the centre that knows how to work with specific tools. There could be challenges with the capacity and prioritization (and potentially motivation) of team members. However, on the other hand, the team should be very aware of all consequences, limitations, and obstacles connected with the tool usage (a good example would be required documentation).

The federated approach is more self-service oriented. The project is responsible for finding the right person for implementation. This means great flexibility, as we can look at the experts on the market; on the other hand, there may be significant challenges connected with the concrete deployment of the tool within the company. Due to this, we can find it very difficult to understand all the processes around the tool ahead of time, so it could be challenging to make any estimates (both from the time and cost perspective).

As you can see, both approaches have their advantages and disadvantages. We just need to realize which mode is used for which tool and realize the risks behind it.

Industrialization process

The industrialization process is about moving from an ad-hoc to a robust solution from an IT perspective. Unfortunately, this is usually not very straightforward and could mean complete reimplementation. Understanding how this is done could therefore help us understand the overall IT risk.

TRY TO ANSWER THE FOLLOWING QUESTIONS:
- [ ] *Is the tool supported? Does the support also extend to added custom components?*
- [ ] *What kind of support is commonly available – infrastructure, data, analytics model?*
- [ ] *Is monitoring established?*
- [ ] *Is there a single support contact for the projects?*
- [ ] *Is there any limitation in the tool usage? Are components missing in the tool in comparison with the market offer?*
- [ ] *How quickly can you get access to the tool? What is the approval process?*
- [ ] *What are the development processes that need to be followed?*
- [ ] *What are the deployment processes that need to be followed?*
- [ ] *Is there a central team that oversees the deployment?*
- [ ] *What is the required documentation? Is an example of the documentation available?*
- [ ] *How much involvement of a central team in the development is needed? Is there a competence centre that could help?*
- [ ] *What is the tool lifecycle, and what is the update roadmap?*
- [ ] *Does the tool support version control, and is version control in place?*

1.3.5   The number of tools paradox

As we briefly discussed, there will probably always be a need to decide the number of tools that will be used for delivery. Two approaches could be challenging to balance (and it could be challenging to understand all the consequences of such a decision at the beginning of the analytics journey). The first approach is to use as few tools as possible. The logic behind this is to limit the knowledge needed, and the integration required. Another approach is to use specific tools for specific tasks – as these tools should be able to meet all the requirements in the respective area without any compromise. These directions are mutually exclusive, so we will need to compromise (everything that was written in this chapter). However, as in every single compromise, we will be forced to give up something – and we need to be ready to explain the consequences of such a choice.

The visualisation of this problem is slightly challenging to read. To highlight the paradox, we have used a visualisation combining two charts. The first (red) one shows complexity in combination with the number of tools. The second (green) one focuses on the relations within the flexibility and number of tools (be aware, that the y-axis has an opposite orientation). This approach helps to highlight the intersection. You can see the visualization in Figure 1.11.

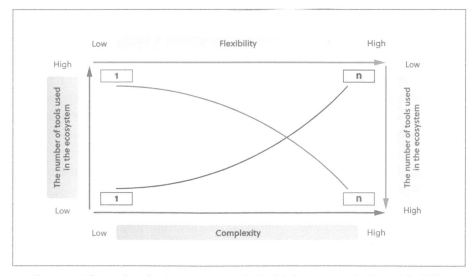

Figure 1.11: The number of tools paradox: the relationship between complexity and flexibility

The intersection of lines is probably the optimal option. It is difficult (or even impossible) to draw this picture realistically (due to the slope of lines), but it can show us a way of thinking that we can follow.

IT standards could define the foundation of the tools – this should serve as our baseline. If we consider adding more tools to the ecosystem, it may be good to understand what kind of problem that will solve for us (what kind of tasks we cannot perform easily in the existing toolset). This approach could help us rationalize every additional tool we would like to include in the solution. Moreover, we do not need to have all tools available from the beginning – we just need to understand which use case should initiate a discussion about adding another piece into the system.

Sometimes, even custom development is considered – creating a specific SW to cover a specific project need. We have opened the debate on the flexibility of tools already – but this is something different. This time it is not about adding additional visualization into the reporting tool; it is about creating a reporting tool to meet specific requirements. In such a case, we recommend considering such an approach thoroughly, for two reasons:

—   The industry has been developing tools for data analytics projects
       for years now. There may be a requirement so specific that it is
       not covered, but maybe it is because we defined the requirement
       wrongly (as it seems we are the only ones who want it).
—   By starting custom development to such an extent, we move out of
       the data analytics project boundaries (and more towards software
       engineering). All three axes described in this book should be
       managed differently for such a project, not to mention the ways
       of working. This will bring new complexity into the system.

IT maturity determines architecture and borders (ad-hoc or robust). IT maturity has a significant impact on many aspects, depending on the company's standards and processes, from flexible onboarding of new technologies and approaches to complex evaluations and proof of concepts or architectonical discussions across various teams or divisions. This applies mainly in the cases of robust solutions using new and untested concepts. Such cases simply bring us to the edge of risk, and potential failure may affect many aspects like time, costs, complex solution lifecycle, and operations.

Tool availability is as just as important, both in ad-hoc and robust projects. It is evident that for ad-hoc projects, we cannot deal with tool integration and processes defined on higher levels. We can use what we can and just implement as delivery is more important for this type of project than the way it is implemented. Tool integration and having good processes in place are more critical for industrialising ad-hoc projects or implementing robust projects from scratch. So, for ad-hoc projects, we expect and support a high level of tool flexibility. We can afford it as we do not need to focus on integration, and it allows us to overcome potential analytics challenges quickly. In robust projects, we can see the opposite direction as integrating tools is much more important (Figure 1.12).

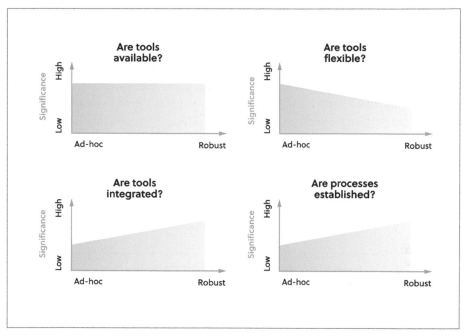

Figure 1.12: The importance of IT maturity factors can vary for ad-hoc and robust projects

To summarize the IT maturity landscape – having the tool available at the company is just a first step on a long journey. We need to understand much more to ensure that we have all the necessary IT support for delivery. Once again, the type of the project (in this case, both the type of analytics and project time frame) is critical for the IT landscape evaluation.

1.3.6 Connection with the type of analytics and time frame

The project time frame could be misleading in IT. One interpretation could be that no IT landscape is needed for ad-hoc projects. However, with the democratization of data and focus on a self-service environment, the opposite could be true. We can see many tendencies to provide an IT solution for the ad-hoc type of project – to support end-users with experimentation without including IT experts. We also need to watch for boundaries (limitations) distinguishing between the IT ad-hoc and robust IT standards. The ideal situation is having a frictionless way to move from the ad-hoc toolset to the robust toolset – the industrialization process does not take any significant effort (which is, unfortunately, rarely the case).

Let us have a look at the following pictures to see this dependency:

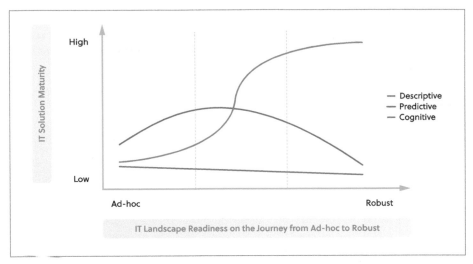

*Figure 1.13: IT maturity development on the journey from
ad-hoc to robust (per type of analytics)*

In Figure 1.13 you can see the overall IT solution maturity (let us aggregate all aspects of IT maturity into one axis). You can see that IT readiness to support the same type of analytics (descriptive, predictive) could differ for the ad-hoc or robust solutions. Due to this, there could be different requirements (or the same requirements addressed differently). The lines for the type of analytics are just demonstrative – and their slope depends on the company's specific IT maturity. In any case, let us describe the three use cases depicted above.

Descriptive

In this case, we have limited IT maturity for the ad-hoc case. It could mean that the IT environment is not able to support a self-service descriptive project. For example, all the processes are very complex and time-consuming or sometimes it may not be possible to provide an environment for a single user. In such cases, people are forced to work with tools that they have natively available (Excel and PowerPoint in most cases). As you move towards a more robust solution, you may find that IT readiness will grow – as there are solid enterprise standards for delivering such projects, but unfortunately, they only start at a certain project size (which is the most common combination for such a project).

Predictive

As predictive projects are conducted in more of an experimentation mode (or at least, it could be the common understanding of such a project), the IT department will have been forced to prepare some environment for ad-hoc projects already. However, if you want to scale it up (move to robust), you may quickly find that it is not ready for the actual robust project, and you will start bumping into obstacles when moving in this direction.

Cognitive

For some companies, this may be an entirely new field. You can potentially leverage an ad-hoc environment for "predictive" projects, but it is not a great fit from the beginning, and you will encounter challenges from early on. There may also be different situations; let us have a look at Figure 1.14.

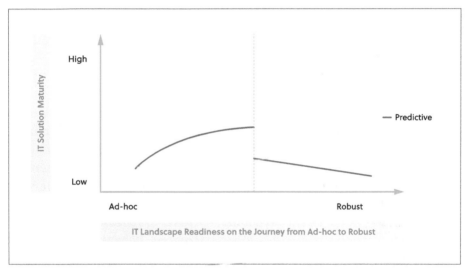

Figure 1.14: IT maturity development on the journey from ad-hoc to
robust – a scenario with a limiting robust environment

What you can see is the obstacle on the way from ad-hoc to robust. There is an environment for ad-hoc development that could have some good features. However, it is not possible to take additional steps in the ad-hoc environment at a certain point. Unfortunately, it is not possible to take them in a robust environment either. That could be a limitation in basically anything – licenses, number of users, performance, data volume, data connection, security, or deployment models... Another even worse limitation is that you do specific work in an ad-hoc environment, but it is not allowed to do it on a larger scale (robust environment) due to specific risks. In this case, the robust environment cannot cover this additional feature which could stop the project work entirely.

There could also be another scenario:

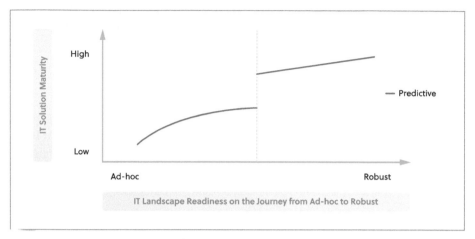

Figure 1.15: IT maturity development on the journey from ad-hoc to robust – a scenario with a limiting ad-hoc environment

In this case (Figure 1.15), an additional step in the ad-hoc environment solution cannot be implemented. To do so, we need to move into a robust environment, which could mean some redesign. For example, some features may be banned in the ad-hoc environment (the volume of data, automatic email alert notifications...), but are easily available in the environment for robust projects. However, there could be conditions that prevent an easy migration to a robust one.

In an ideal world, we should not find ourselves in a situation where we are unexpectedly moving from an ad-hoc to a robust concept. We evaluate the required approach at the beginning of the project (the chapter 1.1 Axis 1: Analytics Maturity), so we should know the right approach. We will have to look at moving from ad-hoc to robust some more in the next chapter (1.4 Ad-hoc x Robust – amplification).

Usually, IT readiness to support different analytics cases depends on the number of such cases in the company (as increasing IT readiness means some investment, so economies of scale apply). Unique cases, therefore, have a more limited IT readiness. Sometimes, it could mean that innovative cases (often unique or requiring a new way of thinking) could be challenging to implement due to low IT maturity. Alternatively, we can say that innovative analytics cases are usually about the analysis itself and the improvement (investment) for the IT landscape.

1.4   Ad-hoc x Robust – amplification

The difference between ad-hoc and robust approaches resonates throughout the three-axis description. That is why we decided to summarize this concept in a specific chapter. We have even considered portraying this difference on another axis, but in the end, we found that it is overly interconnected. We should be able to define whether we are working on an ad-hoc or robust solution at the very beginning – mainly as part of the analytics maturity evaluation, together with the type of analytics. However, this decision is critical for further project evaluation. It is a crucial input for discussing the other two axes (Data and IT Maturity). Let us look at some examples of how this decision influences all three axes (Table 1.1).

	Type of analytics	An example of the ad-hoc approach	An example of the robust approach
Analytics	Descriptive	The stakeholder is provided with ad-hoc report snapshots/ exports for the most relevant dimension combinations	The stakeholder is provided with reporting solution with the option to explore all available combinations of dimensions interactively
	Descriptive	Ad-hoc data discovery for highlighting the sales impact for the selected product	Regular reporting for highlighting sales impact sliced by products
	Predictive	One-time analysis of a sales prediction	An analytical framework for sales prediction, which can be run regularly
	Predictive	Predictive analytics code written without documentation; modelling standards not defined/followed	Advanced analytics code documented, modelling standards defined and followed
IT	Descriptive	A report done in a self-service BI environment with no support and no data refresh automation	A report built in the standard BI environment with automated data refreshes
	Descriptive	Data transformation is done manually in a database or the reporting environment	ETL pipelines are implemented and automated
	Predictive	Advanced analysis run on a data scientist's laptop	Advanced analysis run in the supported modelling environment
Data	Descriptive	The data model is not created; database structures are created as needed	Database development is data model-driven
	Any	Data acquired as an export from the reporting tool or source system	Data acquired from agreed and trusted consumer views
	Any	The only subset of data needed is joined for the analysis, with no readiness for future data variations	Full data sets are integrated; join conditions reflect future data variations known at this time
	Any	The team understands the data, but the descriptions are not documented	Data are described (metadata are captured) in the standard metadata management tool

Table 1.1: Ad-hoc vs Robust approach – examples for all three axes and various types of analytics

Unfortunately, the situation may not be as straightforward. There are a couple of concepts that we need to consider.

First, the decision about ad-hoc or self-service is not necessarily black and white. Often, we will be somewhere in the middle. Imagine that you are conducting an ad-hoc analytics project – and you gain amazing results from it. Then it is highly probable that the push for industrialization (repetitive analysis) will be significant. Therefore, if we (ideally with stakeholders) consider the probability of industrialization in the future from the onset of the project, we can start thinking about following some robust concepts from the beginning. We therefore need to balance how much the robust concept will slow us down within the ad-hoc development.

Moreover, we can consider ways to accelerate the robust development with ad-hoc concepts. In both cases, we need to talk with the stakeholders and explain the trade-off. It is also possible that we will balance it differently for different components of the solution. A typical example is differing approaches for reporting and advanced analytics concepts or robust data preparation (as data can be reused) and ad-hoc advanced analysis. However, it can be even more granular. For example, we may be forced to address security concerns in-depth, although we are doing just ad-hoc solutions (for many reasons – potential reusability for different projects or compliance requirements are some of them).

Second, some data may be available in a robust way. It could be easier to approach them in a very standardized manner than just try to do ad-hoc downloads. Alternatively, some data could be on the industrialization roadmaps of different projects. It could be worth waiting a bit to gain access to the right data, rather than solve everything ourselves (data access, security). Furthermore, this small trade-off may significantly limit the industrialization risk (in case industrialization happens) in the future.

Third – the same as with data, but for the IT landscape. We can have a different toolset available for ad-hoc solutions and robust solutions. The robust IT framework is usually more limited, or more patterns need to be followed. This usually means the development will be slower – but not necessarily. It could be only about the skillset needed and the discipline we have during the development. To reiterate, this may slow down delivery, but it will speed up industrialization in return. The same could be said about the analytics method. For example, following the code standards for ad-hoc projects (even though it is run only on a personal computer) could be beneficial at the end of the day.

The recommendations ought to be evident from the text above. There are a couple of steps to follow:

1. Use a fully ad-hoc approach for purely ad-hoc projects.
2. Use as robust an approach as possible if the delivery time is the same as for ad-hoc.
3. Use a robust approach in the case that it does not significantly prolong

the delivery time but may speed up future industrialization significantly. Always evaluate and explain the trade-off in such a situation.

4.   Avoid the robust concept that will kill the quick ad-hoc delivery.

A basic visualisation that depicts the situation above:

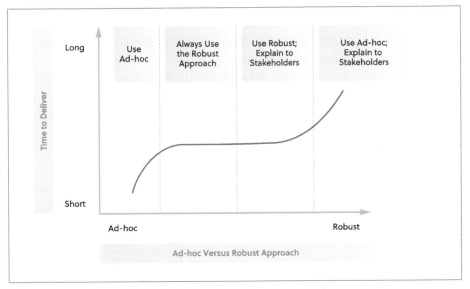

Figure 1.16: The decision on when to use the ad-hoc versus the robust approach depends on the delivery time

The chart in Figure 1.16 could help us understand when it is worth using a robust approach. The blue line depicts the time needed to deliver the project based on the mode of delivery – will we use the ad-hoc or robust approach (the line could differ based on the maturity of axes – mainly IT, but also Data)? The robust approach in this figure means that the solution is reusable (following multiple standards).

You can also see three vertical lines dividing the figure into four main blocks. The first one ("Use Ad-hoc") is for purely ad-hoc projects. After all, it does not make sense to do very quick analyses robustly. A good example would be a 5-minute analysis that I can do in Excel. The second block ("Always Use the Robust Approach") is for projects that can be delivered in an Ad-hoc or a Robust environment at the same time. The next box ("Use Robust; Explain to Stakeholders") is for a situation in which the robust approach requires additional time, but it is not significant (so, it could be still beneficial to use the robust approach). The last box ("Use Ad-hoc; Explain to Stakeholders") is for cases in which the robust approach requires more time, which could be hard to explain (calculate the rentability of investment). The size of all four boxes depends on the curve of the blue line. The curve itself will differ from one company to another. However, we believe that Figure 1.16 represents most cases.

In Figure 1.17, we have added the probability of industrialization. The green line defines the likelihood that the project will be industrialized later – meaning we will need to move from the ad-hoc delivery to robust. This line does not need to continue in the real world, so the visualization is more about conceptual thinking.

You can see the critical decision point represented by the cross of the blue and green lines (the probability of industrialization) – which basically defines the ideal (good balance delivery between time and solution robustness) combination. Additionally, the communication strategy needs to be changed as it should cover only the box close to the decision point.

Let us have a look at two model examples. In our first example (see Case 1 in Figure 1.17), the probability of industrialization is relatively high. In that case, it is primarily worth investing in a robust approach because it pays off as industrialization is highly likely in the future, and we should advise stakeholders accordingly. However, we should avoid an overly robust approach (behind the vertical line) because the delivery time would be too long and not justifiable. The ideal balance between robustness and delivery time lies in the intersection of the two lines.

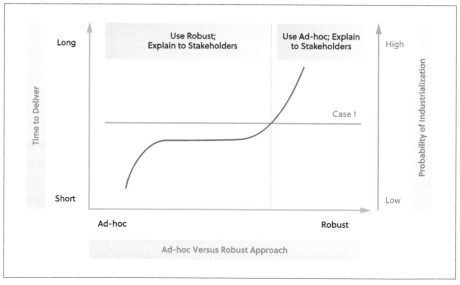

Figure 1.17: When to use the ad-hoc versus the robust approach –
a scenario with a higher probability of industrialization

In our second example (Case 2 in Figure 1.18), the probability of industrialization is lower. Then, in such a model example, the recommendation would always be "Use Ad-hoc" or "Use Ad-Hoc; Explain to Stakeholders," respectively. If the time to deliver a robust solution is greater than the probability of industrialization, then it is not practical to invest in a robust approach.

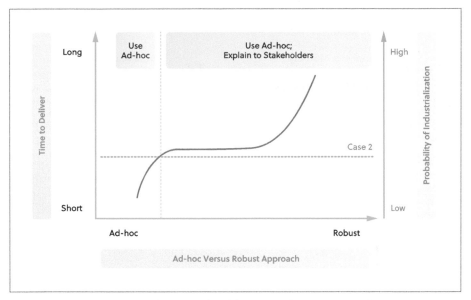

Figure 1.18: When to use the ad-hoc versus the robust approach –
a scenario with a lower probability of industrialization

You can look at each of the examples as a snapshot of one point in time. The project illustrated as Case 1 could have been the same situation illustrated as Case 2 in the past. The project could have easily started as ad-hoc with a low probability of industrialization (Case 2), but when the industrialization probability increased (Case 1), the situation had to be re-evaluated.

Based on the examples above, you can see a different approach must be used based on the probability of industrialization and the shape of the curve that represents the dependency between time and the robustness of the solution. As the project evolves in time (the chapter 3.4 Time impact is dedicated to this topic), the situation could change, and a different approach may need to be chosen. There are always four basic blocks for consideration, but you need to select an up-to-date communication strategy because of your concrete situation. Later, as you move on the curve (you may need to implement a more robust strategy), you can move to a different block.

What is important to realize is the discussion that needs to happen with stakeholders in any case. Either you need to explain the extra time needed for delivery and the benefits that it could bring, or you need to explain that you are not taking any extra time, but there will be risks in future.

Also, as mentioned, an ad-hoc or robust approach could be applicable for all three axes (Figure 1.19), so different approaches will probably be applied for different axes. This increases the complexity of the system of delivery and stakeholder management.

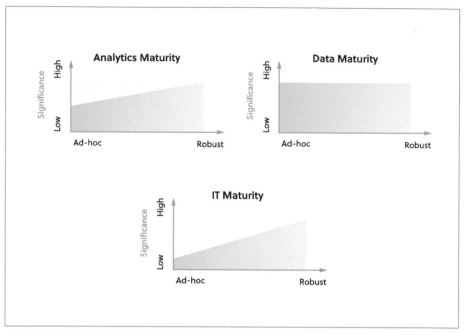

Figure 1.19: *The significance of each type of maturity can vary for ad-hoc vs robust projects*

TRY TO ANSWER THE FOLLOWING QUESTIONS:
- [ ] *Is it an ad-hoc problem?*
- [ ] *Is it an ad-hoc need?*
- [ ] *How likely is it that the same problem/question will need to be addressed next month?*
- [ ] *In case you can have the same analytics support available regularly, would it make sense for you?*
- [ ] *Is the analytics problem significant enough to invest money into automation?*
- [ ] *Do you expect that running the analysis next time will be easier and quicker? Why do you think so?*

1.5   Three axes combined and typical projects

In the text above, we focused on the three axes separately. As we mentioned, there is no universally good position on any axis. Or, more precisely, the position on a specific axis does not necessarily indicate a problem. What we need to do as a next step is combine these axes and start to evaluate the project from a broader perspective – in the context of all three attributes. Also, do not forget about the ad-hoc versus robust project categorization. It is important to have this categorization in mind even though it is not represented by a (another) specific axis (but it is covered in each of them).

1.5.1 Combination of three axes

Now, let us have a look at a simple visualisation (Figure 1.20). Analytics maturity will be axis x, IT maturity will be axis y, and Data maturity will be represented by axis z. Analytics maturity is visualised as "Descriptive → Predictive" as we can simplify it in that way (see chapter 1.1 Axis 1: Analytics Maturity); other axes have "Low → High" as a measure. Combining these three axes creates a cube that can serve as a helpful structure for categorising analytics projects.

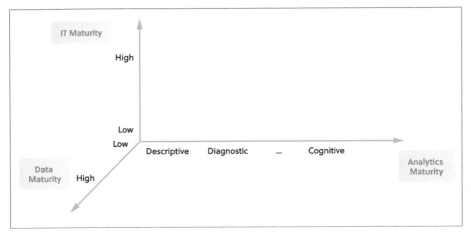

Figure 1.20: Analytics, IT and Data Maturity axes combined in one chart

Based on the work done during the project categorization activity, you should be able to take any analytics project and place it somewhere in the cube (Figure 1.21). Vice versa, you can select any spot in the cube and based on that, you could describe key features of the analytics projects.

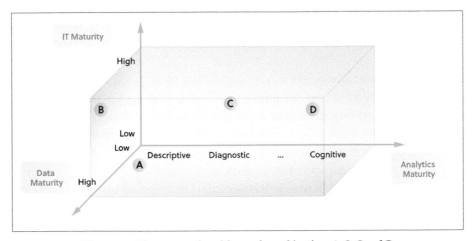

Figure 1.21: Three axes cube with sample combinations A, B, C and D

71

Let us look at a few examples of combinations in the chart (Table 1.2).

	Analytics Maturity	IT Maturity	Data Maturity	Comment
A	Low	Low	Low	The simplest possible combination; might be, e.g., an ad-hoc simple Excel report with a simple data set done by a business professional; it likely would not be considered an analytics project
B	Low	High	High	A typical robust reporting project
C	Medium	Medium	Medium	An advanced analytics solution which can be repeated, though likely with some or many manual operations
D	High	High	High	Automated and integrated cognitive solution with high data maturity. A dream vision for many executives and data scientists

Table 1.2: Sample combinations of various maturity levels

1.5.2 Typical projects

As it is clear from the above examples, not all combinations are equally common and relevant. Some are extremely rare. Some are common but do not translate into analytics projects. Hence it is effective to narrow down our focus on combinations which represent typical analytics projects.

Let us go through the set of the following visualizations to understand the overall combination of axes. Compared to the previous visualization, we need to include the Time Frame perspective (ad-hoc x robust) to understand typical projects better.

Industrialization is most often justified for descriptive use cases; not every advanced analytics project goes robust

This is based on the advanced analytics definition. Most projects focus on ad-hoc analyses trying to solve concrete problems. As soon as we tackle these, we have an answer and a direction for dealing with concrete situations. Some typical examples are industrialized often: sales prediction, marketing campaign optimization, or retention. On the other hand, many analytics problems do not have this character.

Another reason is again hidden in the advanced analytics type of the work as such – it is experimental in nature. It is perfectly OK to end up in a situation where a specific model does not work, or the prediction is not precise enough to go forward. Again, this means that the project will end in the ad-hoc stage.

As we described in the chapter 1.1 Axis 1: Analytics Maturity, the stages are dependent on each other, and e.g., you will likely not build an automated and inte-grated diagnostic solution if there is no reporting in place. More descriptive robust projects will always exist, however.

Descriptive projects can usually gain funding only if it makes sense to make them into a robust solution. Therefore, scalability and reusability are the main driv-ers for the rentability of investment, which automatically means industrialization.

You can see in Figure 1.22, based on the arguments below – the distribution of ad-hoc x robust projects in correlation with analytics maturity.

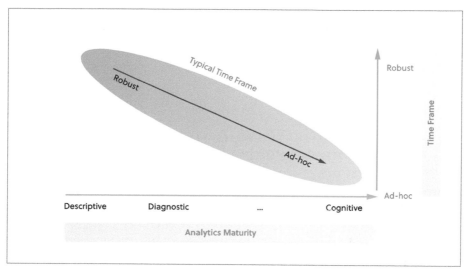

Figure 1.22: Typical distribution of ad-hoc and robust projects
in correlation with Analytics Maturity

IT maturity follows IT investments which go mainly into robust use cases

As IT investments are currently following most cases and reusability, IT maturity follows robust use cases. For the robust use case, it is valuable to prepare an enter-prise environment that deals with common implementation issues.

We still can have an advanced analytics ad-hoc environment ready. However, IT maturity will be lower in comparison with a robust descriptive environment as IT maturity largely depends on reusability and standardization – which is typi-cally low for ad-hoc use cases. So even though the IT maturity for advanced analyt-ics environments could be considered sufficient by users, the overall IT maturity will probably be lower than a robust descriptive environment (support, scalability, security...). From this perspective, we need to realize that this evaluation pertains to the current situation, but a trend could develop in the future (largely depending on market trends as well).

Let us, therefore, add the IT maturity axis in the same figure. We put IT maturity on the same axis as Time Frame. The final visualization is in Figure 1.23.

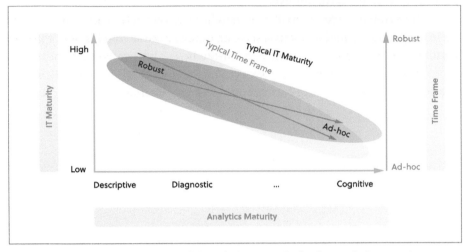

Figure 1.23: The dependency of the typical IT maturity level on analytics maturity

Combination of typical IT maturity and time frame illustrates typical projects

The next step is simply to combine the typical project areas. Combining IT maturity and time frame is a simplification (Figure 1.24), but we can afford it as we are describing typical projects. When evaluating specific projects, we need to stay focused on what is in place and the specifics of each project.

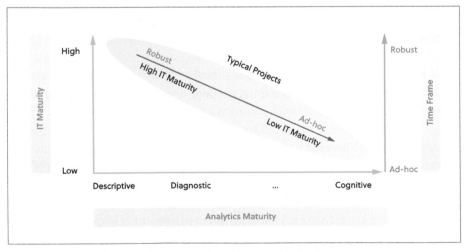

Figure 1.24: The typical distribution of projects with relation to
Analytics Maturity, IT Maturity, and Time Frame

Data maturity decreases for typical advanced analytics projects

An advanced analytics project looks for new insight. One of the easiest ways to gain new insight is to include a new data set as an input. As we are talking about the new data, it is quite probable that data is not described or integrated with the current data set. It could be external data sources, logs, or anything unusual. This could explain the movement on the Data axis. See the final visualisation of a typical project in Figure 1.25.

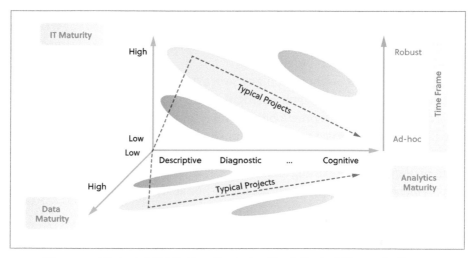

Figure 1.25: The typical distribution of projects with relation to all three maturity axes

The wider area of typical projects goes from higher IT maturity (Robust Time Frame), higher data maturity and lower analytics maturity on the left towards advanced analytics, lower IT maturity (Ad-hoc Time Frame) and lower data maturity on the right. The idea here is that the more you progress in analytics maturity, the less prepared the IT and data environment is.

The spot in the chart at the top right (high analytics and IT maturity) is very attractive and a dream for many professionals as automation, machine learning, and artificial intelligence happen to be hot topics. However, this is very rare as you need to achieve maturity on all axes to hit this golden corner.

On the contrary, the area at the bottom left (low analytics and IT maturity) is very common, but these are not typically framed as analytics projects. E.g., business analysts can do ad-hoc Excel reports or do them regularly every day, but they would not be seen as analytics projects. That does not mean that these activities are not happening – quite to the contrary, they probably account for the most common activities. However, to turn them into a project, one would need a business case, usually hidden in the automation (which automatically brings us higher on the IT maturity axis). This does not mean that no projects focus on building a self-service environment for business analysts. However, this is not in the analytics project category as the result is not mainly generating insight from the data. Therefore, we considered this an IT project (as it improves IT maturity).

1.5.3   Three-axis evaluation and project life cycle

In the beginning, we said that the book's focus is on the initiation phase of analytics projects – project definition, planning, scoping – basically activities that take place before the project (or any new project increment) has started.

Three-axis evaluation – for which we hope we have equipped you by now – happens mainly as part of the Initiation phase but directly or indirectly impacts all other phases of the project life cycle.

In Figure 1.26, we show the life cycle of a typical project or one project/product increment. The concept applies across delivery approaches; more agile delivery approaches would have shorter loops. However, not all phases are equally relevant for all analytics projects. Some phases for some projects can be very straightforward (e.g., the design phase in the case of expanding on existing reporting solutions with no impact on the existing architecture and design) or even skipped (e.g., the deployment and maintenance phases for ad-hoc analysis, which are not released anywhere).

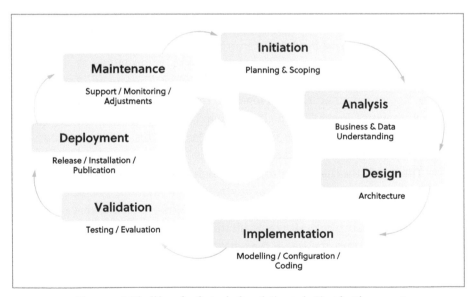

Figure 1.26: The life cycle of a typical analytics project/product increment

In Figure 1.27, we have highlighted the major impacts from the three-axis evaluation on the project phases.

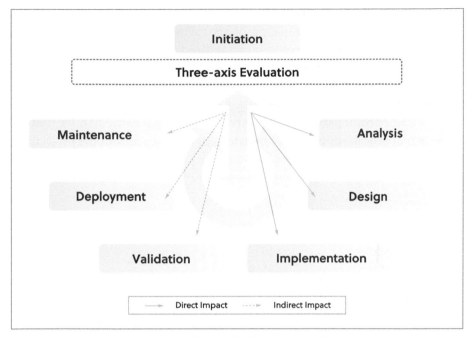

Figure 1.27: Major direct and indirect impacts of the overall three-axis evaluation on project phases

The impact of the three-axis evaluation outcomes on project phases is in Table 1.3.

Phase	Type of Analytics	Time frame (Ad-hoc x Robust)	Analytics Maturity	Data Maturity	IT Maturity
Analysis					
Design					
Implementation					
Validation					
Deployment					
Maintenance					

▨ Direct Impact   ▨ Indirect Impact

Table 1.3: Major direct and indirect impacts of the individual outcomes of the three-axis evaluation on project phases

In general, the three-axis approach impacts every single stage of the project. It should be part of the analytics and design phase of the project as these are the phases in which the project is "defined and set up". It means there is a direct link to the analytics project categorization and understanding of analytics project complexity on any of the three axes. The implementation itself significantly depends on the results of project categorization and on the ability to follow agreed-upon assumptions and approaches (for example, ad-hoc or robust) during the implementation itself. Because of that, we still see the impact as direct. For the last two stages (deployment and maintenance), there are consequences, but these are not so critical – that is why we see them as an indirect impact (as mentioned, these two phases could be even skipped for some types of projects).

An important part is the uninterrupted circle. It demonstrates that the three-axis approach should not be used only at the beginning of the project, but that constant evaluation is needed.

Part two
The Framework in Context

2 Common attributes of analytics projects

Throughout the book, we reiterate that each analytics project is different. At the same time, analytics projects have a lot in common, and these features make them unique compared to other projects. Describing these commonalities could move us further in the conceptual understanding of analytical work. These specific features impact the entire project lifecycle, and neglecting them (trying to use general approaches without tailoring them to analytics projects) can lead to failure.

The commonalities mentioned below are important to some extent for all the types of analytics projects described above. It is difficult to generalize, but we believe you can find at least some in every single type. Being aware of these commonalities could be helpful, as we consider them one of the differentiators of analytics projects. Other types of projects (for example, software engineering development) could have them as well, but they are not crucial, and they are usually evaluated in a different context (that gives them a different level of importance and potential impact). For example, data (we will discuss data focus in the chapter 2.2 Data-driven) are basically used in any project. If you are creating a mobile application, you will need a lot of data (usually, you will generate them as well). However, as the goal of the application is defined from the beginning, you do not depend on data as much as the analytics project (unless the application is an analytics application; then the challenges could be the same). In an analytics project, data are key and define the success of the project. Data need to be there for a mobile application, but the user experience could be more critical.

The commonalities are most prominent on the biggest projects – the bigger the project (scope, team, analytics problem), the greater the impact of commonalities or the importance of understanding the typical characteristics of the analytics project. On the contrary, if the project is delivered just by one person in one tool (which could be perfectly okay), you will find that the commonalities may not necessarily matter as much (in comparison with different project types of a similar scale). In other words, if we neglect commonalities for a smaller project, the impact may not be as significant. Therefore, we decided to emphasise mainly bigger projects in our description – for smaller-scale projects, you can leverage simplification. Of course, the simplification itself depends on the type of complexity and commonality – is it about the team size, business problem complexity or processes within the company?

The commonalities appear in many different areas – change management, project delivery, stakeholder management... The chapter does not delve deeply into addressing these aspects in general (as every area is a broad topic in itself), but the focus is to highlight concrete points that deserve more emphasis on analytics projects. For these, a primary direction could be proposed as a starting point.

2.1   Agile x Waterfall approach

We touch on the agile and waterfall approaches in this book quite frequently. This book should not be about the methodology for delivering the project, but it is impossible to completely ignore the delivery mode as it is closely connected with many areas mentioned. We believe that there are specific "features" of analytics projects that influence this aspect.

Waterfall approach

It is not possible to deliver analytics projects effectively in a waterfall method. It is usually impossible to describe all the requirements for analytics results in advance, as an analytics solution is a journey that changes based on the outputs we see. We need to collaborate with business people closely, show the results, and iterate around them. The delivery team needs to be flexible and proactive. The prototyping phase, especially, is crucial – and in this phase, the delivery team is taking the initiative and designing outputs without any (or with only limited) requirement description.

Some specific projects seem to have requirements described from the beginning (a typical representation of this category is regulatory reporting). But even such a project will have many iterations with business stakeholders and many possible ways to reach the results. Therefore, the iterative approach is ideal.

Agile approach

Agile is the right way to go. However, we need to be aware of three specific aspects that could bring additional complexity into the agile driven project in comparison with others:

— Analytical work is crucial – analysis needs to happen and is always included in everyday tasks. It is not possible (or it is challenging) to analyse the data at the beginning and set up all the work based on the result of the analysis. On the other hand, the analysis result could change the work concept or even the technical solution. This constant uncertainty forces the project team to balance the analytical work that could be done before any planning (regardless of how long) and accept the risk that a significant redesign will be needed if we find new facts based on a later analysis. This balance is difficult to strike, and we need to have very experienced people on the team capable of evaluating and explaining the risk. From some perspectives, 80% of the work is analytical work that is constantly happening during the development.

— Data Preparation – there are dependencies in data preparation work (typically, there is a flow: identify data source → ingest data → prepare data → consume data). There could be shortcuts, but those usually mean generating technical debt. Therefore, it is challenging to create an independent team as the dependency lies in the data, not in the way of working.

— Technical complexity – multiple IT platforms are used for the delivery of a single project. The team is generally composed of different technical specialists who probably cannot quickly work in other technical areas. This could again cause dependency in the teams, which could be challenging for agile delivery.

As we have said, this book is not about how to deliver a project itself – we have simply tried to highlight some aspects of the delivery approach, which cut through the entire book. We have dedicated time to some of these topics in chapter 3.2 Ways of working – WoW.

In general, agile is the right direction. However, we need to focus on reflecting the particulars of analytics projects into the agile methodology and not changing the analytics concepts (derived from the data work characteristics and the analytical work characteristics) to fit them into the methodology.

2.2 Data-driven

Typical data analytics projects are data-driven, not feature-driven. As defined above, a data analytics project improves decision-making by bringing or creating insight from data. Data is the key word in the definition. Therefore, most of the requirements are data requirements (e.g., I want to see calculation ABC in the report...), not functional (e.g., I want to see this box when I click this button, and I want to get an email notification when XYZ happens). The critical value is in the data (not in other improvements), which should drive the project decisions (prioritization of features, sequence of activities, way of working etc.).

To illustrate the way of thinking, imagine two analytics outputs. The first output is a report produced in a modern BI tool with multiple charts and offer filtering per many dimensions. It does not contain any data, however. The second output is a simple report, one table in Excel, but it shows data (assuming they are correct and relevant). The second report brings more value. In analytics, features without data are useless.

There are projects for which the value proposition is "just" to bring data into the central storage (low analytics maturity, high IT maturity). The word "just" is somewhat ironic here as these can be multi-year programmes. The core value is not in the fancy reports but in having the data available (accessible, accurate, described, secure...). Such a value proposition needs to be communicated to the stakeholders.

It might seem that this is true only for reporting projects, but it applies across the cube – for advanced analytics projects, the critical value is not in features, but the calculated data – even a super-advanced algorithm does not bring any value if it does not produce any data.

The fact that analytics projects are data-driven leads to the following implications:

— Project work requires a good understanding of data.
    Development cannot be done without data.
— Data analysis/integration takes the most time (~80%),
    configuration/development is only ~20%.
— What matters is the meaning of data, not the amount. Complexity grows
    with the number of data sources, tables and columns, transformations.
— Correctness of data flows is one of the critical success factors.

Simply said, data are the money that we should generate – or potentially, insight into the data or accessible data.

The data-centric approach also creates a paradox from the WoW perspective. Most of the tasks should revolve around data (as mentioned – approximately

80%). To estimate the complexity of the tasks, you need to understand the data. But the understanding of the data itself is a significant and non-separable part of the task. So, from the WoW perspective – either we will first analyse the data and then define the project task, or we need to accept that the complexity of tasks will be evolving (directly impacting time and money) during the task implementation. Moreover, dividing the tasks into small features may be tricky (it is often recommended as the right approach to managing the complexity) as these pieces depend on each other. Again, if we can divide the work into small pieces, we have already completed a significant portion of the analysis itself.

The increments in an analytics project should be defined around the additional insight that the project could generate. Further insight is provided by having more data available or creating new data using an advanced analytics algorithm. We need to be able to switch to this mindset, and we need to be able to explain it to our stakeholders as well.

To summarize – we need to accept that data rule the analytics project delivery. Not features (nice charts, email notifications...), but data are the key for successful delivery.

2.3   Technology mix

A typical data analytics project leverages IT platforms to create data solutions. Every data analytics project probably has unique data requirements in the context of the company or division; otherwise, it would probably not exist. On the other hand, the technical approach (higher-level IT architecture, tools...) does not need to be unique, and analytics projects usually leverage IT platforms in the company as it usually does not make sense to build the analytics software from scratch.

There are many reasons why it makes sense to leverage analytics IT platforms if they are available, compared to custom engineering from scratch:

—   The most common requirements are faster to deliver. For
    example, achieving requirements for a typical report is much
    quicker in a modern BI tool than custom coding.
—   Knowledge already exists with the platform and delivery teams.
    Delivery teams can benefit from the technical expertise of the central
    team. Moreover, if the platforms are reused on multiple projects,
    delivery teams can benefit from the experience from previous projects.
—   Parts of solutions can be reused across projects. If multiple
    projects use the same platform over time, there can be
    additional synergies – e.g., an advanced configuration can be
    reused if it applies to more frequent analytics use cases.

— Engineering and process support is available – technology is validated for use in the company, documentation processes are set up, there is a support team for the infrastructure etc.

Leveraging platforms has the following implications:

— There are always limitations on the functionality and flexibility in the platform tools (e.g., flexibility for user experience improvements), and therefore some business requirements might not be achievable by the delivery team.
— Custom development can cause problems during upgrades. Because of the limitations in functionality, the delivery team might come up with custom code changes within the platform tools. It might fulfil the business requirements, but the team should watch out for the maintenance of such changes as the change may not be supported in future versions of the analytics software. The business benefit of such custom changes should always be considered – whether it is worth not just the development efforts but also the future risks.
— Regular meetings with platform support teams are needed to evaluate whether the solution under development is not too complex. Again, this is strongly related to the previous team; the delivery teams should be in touch with central platform teams to help stakeholders achieve the right balance between the desired business requirements and the long-term stability/maintainability of the solution.
— Regular meetings regarding platforms are needed to discuss missing features as they are responsible for adding them. The platform team can potentially offer a feature that was missing from the current project for the next project, but they need to hear the feedback and requirements from the business or delivery teams.

If we go higher in IT maturity, it can easily happen that the project is being delivered not just on one platform but across multiple ones. For example, an ingest platform used for loading data, a data storage platform used for storing data, an integration platform used for data extraction and transformation, a master data management platform used for connection to reference data etc. Despite the many benefits of the platforms described above, it significantly increases the complexity of the delivery and support as it requires alignment across many platforms and teams. Such an approach also typically requires multiple specific roles (business analyst, data modeller, ETL developer, report developer, solution architect...), and we will discuss it more in the WoW chapter (3.2 Ways of working - WoW).

While benefiting from platforms is more typical for analytics projects compared to software development projects, there are many valid cases where leveraging IT platforms might not be an option:

— IT platforms are not available in the company at all.
— IT platforms are available, but there are none for the use case (e.g., there is a platform for data preparation but not for data visualization or advanced analytics).
— An IT platform is available for the general use case, but it is impossible to achieve critical business requirements in this technology and custom coding.
— It is not efficient to leverage the platform considering the project scope and value proposition – e.g., an ad-hoc advanced analytics project can begin without leveraging any platform and start to use a platform in the industrialization phase.

If no platform is ready, and we would like to develop the missing pieces of the platform within the project, we need to realize that we are moving outside the bounds of analytics projects. We need to address different problems and be guided by other principles. It is still possible to do so, but it will cause additional complexity.

2.4   Data-oriented thinking and effective client communication

A typical data analytics project requires specific knowledge, data-oriented thinking, and effective client communication skills. An engineer on the analytics project needs to be skilled in the tools used for the projects (and there might be multiple technologies in one project, as mentioned in previous chapters).

As we already highlighted, data (and their analytical enrichment, transformation, calculation, aggregation...) drive business value, which also must be reflected in the engineers' skill set. In addition to technical experience, data analytics projects need professionals with data-oriented thinking. Every engineer on a data analytics project is not just a developer but also an analyst to a certain extent.

By data-oriented thinking, we mean structured and extremely logical thinking in many different combinations with a high level of abstraction. Perhaps it is easier to illustrate it with examples, namely two questions that challenge data-oriented thinking:

— Imagine a theme park (roller coasters, aqua park). How would a data model for a theme park look? What entities and relationships among them would be present and why? What attributes would those entities have? For some people, the term "data model or attributes" may not be clear. To put it more generally, we can say it describes the relations within the theme park. It is worth asking this question to test logical thinking – how would you describe the working relations with the theme park? If we get an answer that will start to categorize various entities, describing their attributes and relations, we are on the right path. You may be surprised that an experienced data modeller will not provide as good an answer as a strictly logical thinker with no experience in data modelling. We are trying to highlight that this is not about professional expertise; it is about the way of thinking that you can apply to data.

— Imagine two large tables – one with emails (transactions) and the second with people (recipients and senders). Think about what attributes these two tables might have and how you would combine them for reporting? The same comment regarding the previous point is valid here as well.

Developers ideally need to be able to answer these questions to some extent. If they cannot, someone else needs to translate the business requirements into the code specification. For this, we may need to have a middle layer used as a communication channel between data analysts and developers. If we think about it in detail: the data analyst could follow the same patterns for such a definition, so we can probably generate the code automatically without developers. That is a trend within both tools and skillsets – so the team will likely consist of more data analysts who can design the code (regardless of how) and deep technical specialists who manage the automatized code generation and focus on complex tasks that cannot be automatized.

We need to highlight one more skill area, and that is effective client communication. You could say that communication is vital for everyone, and we could not agree more. The difference here is that data professionals typically work more closely with the business (more than software engineers) during the development as no one else can answer the questions. Data professionals (data scientists, visualization specialists...) are not only programmers; they communicate with clients, understand their needs, and help shape the scope. It will not do to simply have a generic business analyst in between (or it might, but then we get the same problem as with data analysts and developers). A data professional needs to be able to listen to needs, be consistent in their communication, and be able to manage the scope with all the flavours and specifics of the particular analytics project.

Often in our careers, we have seen that hiring someone with a strong motivation and the ability to learn quickly and think logically and solid communication skills has paid off more than getting a technological expert without this drive to "think data" and the ability to communicate with stakeholders.

2.5   Maintenance of analytics

People can think that after the analytics project is delivered, the solution is released into production, and after a couple of weeks of hypercare, the engineering work is done unless there is a new scope or bugs. This might apply to some software engineering projects but is rarely true for analytics projects. Typical data analytics projects require the maintenance of advanced analytics models and data logic.

Every advanced analytics model works well under assumptions based on current knowledge and the current state of the world. If the assumption or this state changes, they need to be adjusted to the new conditions. It is more common for advanced analytics projects, but it can also be true for descriptive analytics/reporting – the business logic of data flows can change too. For example, new transaction types must be included in the metric calculation; otherwise, the calculations will result in incorrect numbers. Is it a bug? No – the solution behaves as was previously accepted and follows the logic agreed in the past. But regardless of whether it is classified as a bug, change request or minor enhancement, it needs to be changed, assuming the numbers are corrupted otherwise.

Analytical work needs to be monitored and evaluated for changes that might be necessary. The role performing the required changes is traditionally not present in platform support teams; hence, analytics teams need to help maintain the code or configurations. See more in 1.3.4 Are processes established?

2.6   Prototyping and Experimentation

Parts of the analytics project are usually delivered in the "experimental" way of working. This means that it is challenging to define them precisely before the work starts; the scope of the work evolves while work is underway. In general, we see two main categories (three respectively).

Experimentation

This is quite common in the Advanced Analytics area – we only have a definition of the business problem and data. The first goal is to find an analytics method that could help us to find an answer. But it is not clear which analytical approach should be used. The team needs to try a couple of mathematical approaches, potentially including additional data or reformulating the question (or even reformulating the business problem). The result of this work could also be that we cannot address the described problem (no matter the reason). This result should then be respected and accepted by stakeholders.

Sometimes, we see an even vaguer scope. Data are available; could you have a look and try to find some hidden insight? In such a case, we recommend defining the business problem at least on a high level and including business people as much as possible. Otherwise, we can risk wasting resources on finding something obvious from a business perspective or something completely useless. Good cooperation with business people is critical.

A specific type of experimentation could be data discovery tasks. In this case, we are trying to evaluate whether a new data set could bring more value (additional insight) into an analytics project. These could be challenging tasks due to many reasons:

— The new data set is not described (the data maturity of the data set is low)
— The new data set is difficult to integrate within existing data
— The new data set does not necessarily bring the expected analytical value

Data discovery work should be done differently than data integration work as they have different outputs (especially in robust projects). For data discovery, we would like to evaluate the value of the data set as quickly as possible. On the other hand, in data integration work, we would like to have integrated data. Because of this difference, we can even use different toolsets and different WoW.

Prototyping

Prototyping is more common in descriptive projects. We usually know what to visualize, but we do not know how. Then it could be better to iterate around prototypes than spend a great deal of time on the visual definition and then implement it in a visualisation tool. The data visualisation prototyping process could be risky mainly because:

— A change in visualisation could lead to a change in underlying data structures – which could have a significant impact.
— Avoiding the expensive change in underlying data could lead to incorrect usage of the reporting tool, which could cause problems later on (technical debt creation).
— High tool customization could produce the desired visual appearance, but higher maintenance costs usually go hand in hand. Therefore, we always need to consider trade-offs in these cases.
— The data itself (data change) could break the visualisation concept. For example, if we double the number of products we have, we can be forced to change the reporting concept. That could be a challenge if the prototype is done using sample data or even during the report usage (in a production environment).

Another useful type of prototyping could be the mock-up definition. That may be very powerful, but it may also cause a different type of challenges. When we spend a long time creating a mock-up definition in advance without working with a concrete reporting tool, we can find that we cannot even implement the lovely UI prepared by the designers (or the level of customization is too high). Furthermore, without seeing the real data in mock-up, the mock-up definition could be misleading and not necessarily reflect the final results. If you start to consider all aspects of data (like discussed number of products), a mock-up definition could become very complex, and direct prototyping in the reporting tool could be quicker and easier for industrialization later.

Research

We mentioned two categories initially, but research could also be applicable. This is for cases where the project team finds a new mathematical method/model that could be used (or potentially patented). Thus, the result of the effort is not the answer to the business question but a new way to gain this answer. This could have a great value, but usually for different stakeholders.

We believe that highlighting these aspects is vital for two main reasons:

Agile misunderstanding

Usually, everyone will agree that prototyping (experimentation) is a regular part of working in an agile environment. However, the point of agile is to take small steps that bring business value. So that from some perspective, you know from the beginning what the target state is, you know its characteristics, and you are adding the functionality "slowly" (over MVP – minimal viable product concept). A thing that could be different for the analytics project is that you can end up at a dead end. It means that we are not taking small steps that lead directly to the target state, but we are excluding the non-working approaches. Simply put, we might need to start over after two months of effort – knowing only how NOT to do it. That is mainly caused by the "data-driven" characteristics of analytics projects.

With experimentation, prototyping and data discovery, we might need to discuss with stakeholders what we consider the added business value and include steps that are valuable indirectly.

Other parts of the project with a different approach

If we start talking about data preparation and integration, we can find that work is driven differently. We are not prototyping, but we need to handle data correctly from the beginning. Data we prepare may not be used immediately (due to the result of experimentation), but data will be ready for further analysis. Or vice versa – experimentation will confirm the analytics approach, but in order to progress further, proper data feeds will need to be established first. Combining the data and analytics aspects could be difficult, as each uses a different approach.

3 General areas of risks and challenges

Challenges and risks – another critical aspect of analytical initiatives that could be the same from the overall definition perspective, but the realisation and mitigation could significantly differ based on the previously described project categorisation.

In the third chapter, we will look at the specific features of different types of analytics. As we discussed the three-axis approach in detail, it is clear that there is no such thing as a universal type of analytics project with one stable set of issues and one approach that can be followed. At the same time, projects that are close to each other in the cube may have commonalities in the kind of challenges you need to overcome when setting up such a project. Therefore, we will try to map these risks and challenges onto the project categorization.

The relation of the challenges and project scale is the same as for commonalities. Having a large-scale project (size, team, business problem) amplifies the challenges. Again, we decided to describe them mainly for the large-scale project, and it is up to you to use simplifications based on your current situation.

Like the commonalities, the challenges come from many different areas – change management, project delivery, stakeholder management... And like in the case of commonalities, we are not addressing these areas directly. We will only highlight the critical elements that deserve closer attention in the general domain (like change management). Once again, you can take this as fundamental guidance on how to address the described challenges.

3.1   Key challenges in managing stakeholders' expectations

Wrong expectation (or wrongly managed expectation) is one of the most common challenges on any project. Therefore, we would like to highlight the primary sources of challenges in stakeholder management depending on the nature of the analytics project. We found out that overlooking these significant specifics often causes not meeting the stakeholders' expectations, whereas reflecting them is the key for framing a new analytics initiative and one of the enablers for project success in general.

To illustrate these significant challenges, we will simplify our three-axis chart into one axis. We will only keep analytics maturity and IT maturity and focus on typical projects only. That let us translate the model onto a single axis (see Figure 3.1). So now we have typical low analytics maturity & high IT maturity projects on the left and typical high analytics maturity & low IT maturity projects on the right. For the sake of simplicity, we will refer to the part on the left as descriptive or reporting projects and the projects on the rights as advanced analytics.

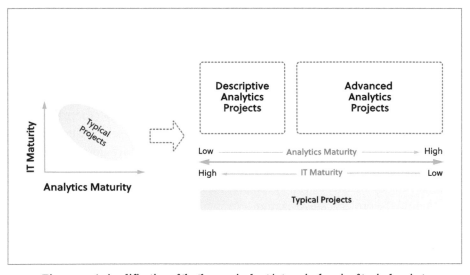

Figure 3.1: A simplification of the three-axis chart into a single axis of typical projects

Two areas vary significantly across this line of typical projects, and we would like to highlight them. Both influence expectation management considerably:

1.   SCOPE DEFINITION – the process of determining the scope, i.e., the agreement on project objectives and what outcomes (deliverables or value) need to be delivered in what timeframe.
2.   PROJECT DELIVERY/IMPLEMENTATION – an actual realization of the scope

3.1.1   Scope definition

The client, not the delivery team, typically leads the scope of reporting projects. The delivery team is usually invited after it is made clear that the decision-making process requires a reporting solution. As we saw in the typical project journey above, clients often already have some ad-hoc reports with the desired data. Or at least they know why they need to measure the data, and the business requirements are relatively straightforward – making the desired data available for decision-making. Note: Though the team usually does not challenge the project objectives of a reporting project, other areas can be initiated by the stakeholders but challenged by the team – e.g., how the report should look or how the metrics should be calculated.

For advanced analytics projects, the situation is quite different. It is next to impossible for stakeholders to define the right scope for such projects alone without involving the delivery team. The experience and knowledge of data science professionals are needed to set the project up reasonably. Without the understanding of analytics methods, the scope can happen to be just an unfulfillable wish. Business stakeholders bring general objectives and priorities, but experienced data scientists with a knowledge of the "art of the possible" should help shape the scope and produce the project's deliverables.

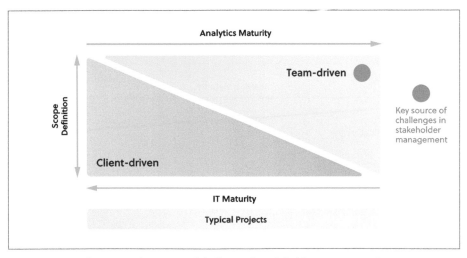

Figure 3.2: A key source of challenges in stakeholder management for advanced analytics projects is in the scope definition area

Note: We are excluding data maturity for simplicity here, but this by no means reduces its importance. Data availability and its understanding can be a game-changer in scope definition. If data are not available to support the desired scope of an advanced analytics initiative, the objective will not be achieved even if analytics methods would allow it to be fulfilled.

The fact that the scope of advanced analytics projects should be driven by the data science team and not the client is the key source of challenges in managing the stakeholders' expectations for advanced analytics projects (Figure 3.2). In reporting projects, sometimes the delivery team wants to drive the report definition too much, even though it is not a critical part of the project. We can see a massive focus on the visual appearance of reports, which is potentially not the most important piece of work that needs to be done (we are not saying that it is not important at all, though).

3.1.2   Project delivery/implementation

Though the scope definition introduces more challenges for advanced analytics projects, project/delivery implementation is more straightforward for such projects from the perspective of managing stakeholders' expectations. That is because the core of the work is coding the data science algorithms, and business stakeholders typically have at least a rough idea about the complexity and understanding of the time and resources needed to deliver the outcomes.

For reporting projects, the type of work is quite different. There might be no coding, only frontend configuration and data analysis, and data integration is what takes most of the time.

Complexity grows with the number of data sources, tables and columns, and transformations, not necessarily new features as there might be no feature requirements.

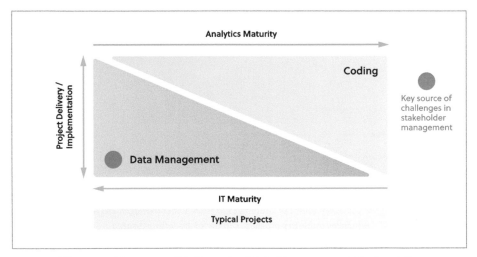

Figure 3.3: A key source of challenges in stakeholder management for descriptive analytics projects is in the project delivery/implementation area

With reporting projects, teams can easily find themselves in a situation where everyone agrees on what needs to be delivered, but the client does not understand why it takes so much time to do so. Analysis of the data sources, communication with data stewards, data modelling, resolving data quality issues, testing integrated data pipelines for various combinations – all these are examples of instrumental activities which can be invisible for the business stakeholders but can easily take weeks or months, up to 80% of the delivery time.

Quite a typical situation where expectations need to be managed appropriately: the delivery team shows the dashboard configured in a modern BI tool with embedded ad-hoc data. The client loves the dashboard as it follows the requirements and gets the impression that the project is near completion. But to industrialize the dashboard, make it repeatable, integrate it with other components of the analytics landscape etc., can take a couple more weeks or months.

Since the delivery of low analytics maturity/high IT maturity projects is mainly about data management activities, the key source of challenges in managing the stakeholders' expectations for descriptive analytics/reporting projects is in the project delivery/implementation area (Figure 3.3).

3.1.3   Connection with stakeholder expectation

We have discussed the scope definition and the implementation process – but how is this connected with stakeholder management? We believe that these two factors are critical for defining the relationship with stakeholders and the style of communication that we need to choose. For example, if there is a stakeholder that only has experience with one type of project and therefore expects that another project will run in the same way (even though it is a different type of analytics), we can be sure that there will be many discussions and misunderstands on the way. So, to translate the scope and implementation into the stakeholder problems, let us try to summarize them into the following points:

— How quickly and easily can we change the scope?
  How much flexibility do we have to change the scope?
— How much should we be included in evaluating the results during the project (remember that expectations could be wrong in both extremes – too much or too little)?
— How much time will be needed in general?
— How much time will be needed for specific steps?
— How will the work be done in general?
— How much does the work depend on data automation?

Answering and discussing these questions with stakeholders will help us adequately explain the critical parts of projects. Ideally, this should lead to setting the expectations correctly.

3.2   Ways of working — WoW

In the beginning, we said that we would not be talking about the implementation itself. However, understanding how the work will be organized and potentially how the team will be structured is undoubtedly helpful. Again, there are many ways to do it; none is 100% right for every situation. As in the previous chapter (3.1 Key challenges in managing stakeholders' expectations), we will have a look at it from a different project perspective.

WoW is a combination of many factors for us, and each could be described in a separate book. In general, it is about the way the project is delivered. It could be as high-level as project delivery methodology, project team organization or the balance between experimentation and well-defined work. Simply put, it is anything connected with the project delivery itself. As usual, we will have a look at this aspect from the analytics project perspective.

Before we dive into the different examples, let us quickly look one more time at the agile way of working specifically. We have already introduced the comparison of agile and waterfall in a separate chapter (see 2.1 Agile x Waterfall approach) but let us look specifically at their impact on WoW. Currently, there is a big focus on agile, and the agile approach is used on every single project – and it is a good step forward, as agile is more of a methodology on how to run a project in general. On the other hand, agile will not help us in concrete situations. Or, more precisely, agile will not help us with the concrete characteristics of some data analytics projects. We do not propose following the waterfall methodology. We just need to know how to use the agile approach in different situations and understand the most common challenges that agile (or any methodology) will not be able to tackle. Sometimes challenges are caused by these data analytics project characteristics being wrongly described as a failure due to the project implementation methodology (regardless of whether we blame the waterfall approach or we are not experienced enough in agile). But no methodology will remove these characteristics. So, the right question is how to deal with them properly or incorporate them into the delivery methodology itself.

The three most common challenges that could cause such a misunderstanding are:

1.   Data
2.   Diverse skillset needed
3.   The impact of change

Data

The most representative challenge is the dependence on data. Data are key for analytics projects – you need to have data available basically for every analytical task you would like to do. But sometimes, collecting and preparing data in the right form is the most demanding task (we described it in the chapter 3.1.2 Project delivery/implementation as well). This concept can then cause dependency in the way of working. In agile, ideally, the team should be independent, and tasks (stories, features, epic – depending on the specific vocabulary used) should be possible to deliver in parallel. That is a significant challenge for any project where you need to centralise and integrate data first. Either you will structure the team so that some teams will be waiting for the team preparing data, or more teams will be preparing data at once, which causes a challenge with one integrated data storage. There are techniques for setting up the team and structuring the work to limit the risks (let us look at it in concrete examples), but the most important is to realize it before the work starts.

Diverse skillset needed

In agile, ideally, independent squads are needed. That could mean that every single squad consists of people with all the possible technical skills. At the same time, there is a requirement that people in the squad should be substitutable (which is not possible because of different skillsets). As you can see, this is a paradox that is not easy to solve. There are indeed multidisciplinary people who can cover more tasks, but do we really want to have a data science person capable of writing the data transformation when necessary? And if we have such a person, are they the best in both areas? We have also already highlighted that tools have overlaps. So having one person doing more technical tasks could also mean that we are potentially doing the task in the wrong toolset (which could complicate the deployment later or significantly slow down the solution's performance). To summarize, this challenge is about building delivery squads – focusing on technology (one step on the data journey) or as an independent unit that could cover everything (all steps on the analytics journey). Both could be used, but it is crucial to understand which approach we choose and the possible implications and risks that it could bear.

Currently, most agile trained people (scrum masters, agile couches…) come from software engineering projects (as this is where the agile approach started), or at least agile training is usually based on experience from software engineering projects. However, in this area, the multi-skill technical need is not such a big problem. That could be why this challenge might be underestimated or even not considered at all. However, this is typical for analytics projects, so it is worth keeping it in mind.

Still, we highly recommend focusing on the T-Shape person (a multiskilled person whose experience extends into multiple related regions and can therefore perform a broader range of tasks on the analytics data project). Examples include a data scientist with data engineering skills who can do most of the data preparation tasks and helps to reduce future industrialization efforts; a business analyst who can perform basic data preparation and data visualization activities on their own without needing data specialists; a senior data modeller with ETL experience who can achieve end-to-end data acquisition in a robust data warehouse, and similar.

It is a long-term journey to grow such a person as it requires a unique combination of data skills, technical skills in numerous areas, and business domain skills. We are highlighting that it could be quite risky to expect that these people are automatically available for the project or that it is easy to find them on the market.

The impact of change

Another challenge could be the impact of change on the analysis. One small change in the visualization of data could mean many things:

— Indeed, a small change in the visualization
— A complex change in the visualization (typically the construct of the visualization) although the UI only changed a little
— A change in the underlying data model
— An addition of another data source
— A change of the advanced analytics mode that needs to generate other data
— An E2E change

It looks straightforward, but the problem lies in predictability. If you want to schedule the work for the next sprint (or any time), you need to understand what type of work you will do (is it just a change in visualization or lots of new data). To do that, you need to run a robust business analysis in advance (from another perspective, you need to run a small ad-hoc project) to define requirements. And defining requirements in advance is often not so easily possible, and it is also one of the main features of the waterfall approach. Again, there are strategies for addressing this, but the best one, in general, is understanding this complexity. If everybody is aligned as to what may happen, the team could be ready for it. For example, there could always be some capacity dedicated to the team allowing them to absorb unexpected changes (so you can decrease the complexity of analysis). You can dedicate time to working on business feedback continuously; you can use experimentation/prototyping to help define requirements in advance; or you can even use different methodologies for different teams. For some teams, you can plan the work efficiently for an upcoming couple of weeks, while for other teams, it is not as easy as they are more focused on fixing unexpected changes.

The challenges described above are not present in every analytics project (and their significance may vary), depending on the placement of the project into three axes. Now, let us look at three examples of various analytics projects, focusing on WoW. These examples should represent the most common types of analytics projects, but they are by no means exhaustive. We will be describing a suggested approach for cases when you do not have anything specific in your project that you are aware of from the beginning. It is a good starting point that could be changed later based on the development. Moreover, please remember that we are describing large-scale projects – you can always simplify.

3.2.1   WoW – Advanced analytics ad-hoc project

This is probably the easiest type of project from the delivery model perspective (not to imply it is easy to deliver). The Agile approach could be implemented (and should be implemented) in every part of the work.

Usually, only one type of squad is needed – with both the knowledge of the business problem and data science expertise. They work iteratively in different phases (many methodologies focus on this aspect, such as CRISP-DM). We are just summarizing from a high-level perspective:

1.   Business Statement Definition (a high-level challenge description, for example, "increase revenue")
2.   Problem Definition (a more detailed description of what should be done, for example, "reduce the price")
3.   Data Evaluation
4.   Data Wrangling
5.   Algorithm Creation
6.   Algorithm Evaluation
7.   Presentation of Results

As you can see, the steps follow the data journey logic – which is very straightforward in this case. Everyone understands that the problem needs to be defined (or at least formulated) before we start the analysis. Therefore, usually, there is no discussion about the necessity of some steps (which could be challenging).

We should follow the steps in order as stated so we can go back if we need to re-evaluate the progress we already achieved (in every previous step). This follows the standard way of thinking, so this approach is usually well-received.

There is no cross-team dependence, which substantially reduces the delivery management complexity, as there is only one team. The team is composed mainly of data science people as there is usually no need for any specific technology that the DS people are not familiar with (or it is not considered a DS toolset)

There needs to be someone in the team who can speak with business and understand the business language. That is sometimes underestimated (as the focus is often on Data Science people – mathematicians), but there are critical tasks that need to be covered:

1. Understanding the business problem in the business language (we would like to have a forecast)
2. Translating the business problem into data science language (let us use a time series analysis for a forecast)
3. Explaining the limitation to the business (using a time series will not help us predict unexpected events per the definition)
4. Demonstrating and presenting the results to the businesspeople (what the results mean, how to interpret them, how to use them, what are the real limitations)
5. Business Statement/Problem Definition re-evaluation

Moreover, the business problem definition may change during the analysis. That may be because of the availability of data, a low level of confidence in the model, or just because the data analysis will bring further insight into the data, which will change the approach or focus of the analysis. For example, you can start with a problem defined as a prediction of sales, but you can end up with customer segmentation. From some perspectives, it is still the same problem (as segmentation could help you predict sales), but it is very different from the algorithm and result implementation perspectives. That is another reason why we need to have a close relationship with business (someone who can speak with them) – this is hidden under the last point.

Usually, the IT landscape is not very complex. The team leverages any tool that is comfortable for them and uses it for every step of the solution. As the team is consistent, this approach speeds up delivery and ensures smooth cooperation within the team. However, it does not mean that the tool set used is optimal, and even in such a project, the team could encounter the tool's limitations. This approach requires additional attention for projects where follow-up industrialization is expected. In such a case, selecting the tool used could have a significant impact on the next steps.

A specific type of such a project is "experimentation" (also mentioned in the chapter 2.6 Prototyping and Experimentation). In such a case, the business problem is not defined well (the business statement should be defined at least on a high level). For example, we would like to increase sales (as a business statement), but we do not know how to start or which area we would like to focus on (will we begin to analyse costs or revenue? Will we focus on the customer segment or product optimization?). Therefore, understanding the business side is critical, and collaboration between the delivery team and business people needs to be very close. Otherwise, the delivery team could analyse data and find something that everyone in the business team knows, with the data proving something that is already obvious. Or it could be the other way around – the delivery team could recommend something impossible to do. For example, the result could be placing the product on a particular market, which is impossible due to regulation. Or the recommendation could be to decrease the price, which may not necessarily be possible.

The described WoW is visualized in Figure 3.4.

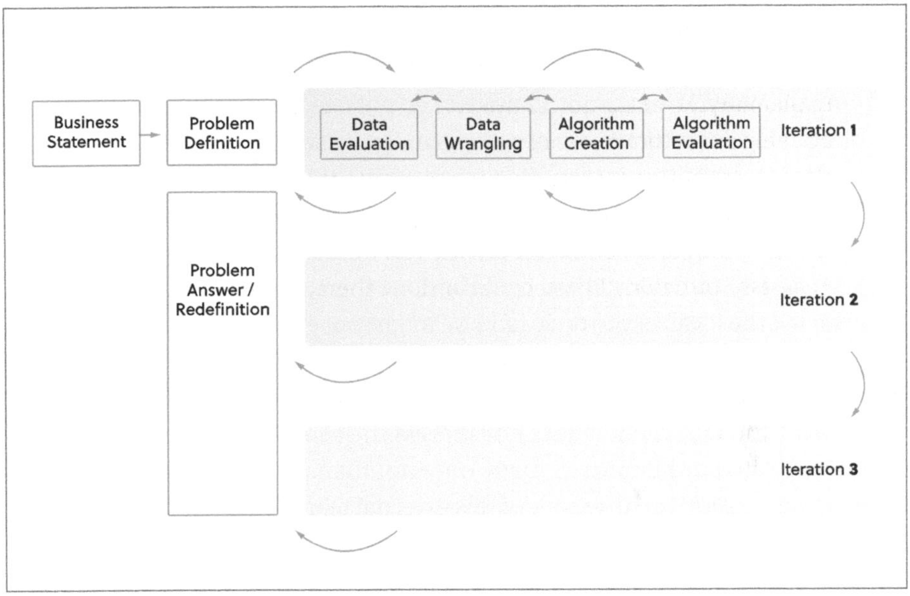

Figure 3.4: The way of working in an ad-hoc advanced analytics project

The team works in steps and iterations (moving back and ahead), regularly talking with business.

For small scale projects, all the above could be easily covered by one person. Still, the delivery process is the same, but one person could cover all the needed roles (especially if the person is from business). That could significantly help as the time usually required for communication, explaining the progress or the business problem or defining the next steps is saved and could be used for development itself.

3.2.2 WoW – Robust descriptive analytics project (data are ready)

Regarding the definition, the way we see this type of project is that a new reporting solution is needed for the business domain that has not been addressed so far. It does not necessarily need to be so strict; the important thing is that it is not just existing reports enhancement. So, a part of the work is, for example, the business domain KPIs definition.

This example is quite rare in reality – although many projects are described in this way. The assumption (and understanding of the stakeholders) is relatively straightforward as well – we just need to take data and create a visualization as data are already available (in a data warehouse). And namely, this assumption could bring much confusion and could impact the delivery.

Let us look at what it can mean that data are ready. Data could be ready in the data warehouse, but are they ready in the structures needed for reporting (from a business or performance perspective)? Moreover, if we need to prepare data to some extent, where will we do so? Answering this question is the foundation for defining the WoW. If we are not allowed (or do not need to) to make any changes in the underlying data storage, we need to form the delivery team differently than if we need to (we are authorized to) make changes in the underlying database. Again, we need to realise that the technical limitations of preparing the data could lead us to use the reporting tool wrong (we discuss this in the chapter 1.3 Axis 3: IT Maturity). Many data transformations could be done there, but that does not necessarily mean it is the ideal way to do so (and we might not even be authorized to do so).

Another approach for limiting the data preparation part is to move it out of the project scope – data are prepared as part of other initiatives. That would help us to clarify the scope, but it does not address the complexity. It will only create dependency on another project that we are not managing, and it could be more challenging to prioritize the scope of this external team.

So, the assumption "Data are ready" could mean some of the following:

—   Data are ready in the correct format.
—   Data are ingested and somehow prepared for reporting,
     but we will need to manage the data transformation in the
     reporting tool to some extent (and we are authorized to).
—   Data readiness is ensured by another team, which
     is out of the scope of our initiatives.

If any of the above is true, we can look at the WoW in such a situation.

There should be more teams working in cooperation on such a project – as we stated at the beginning, we are considering bigger projects as an example (a new reporting area), so multiple teams should be there to speed up delivery. If it is a smaller project, the teams could be structured differently but should have the same competency. First, however, let us have a look at the activity that needs to happen in parallel before we jump into the team definition.

Define all the necessary general concepts that will be valid across the new business domain

This stream should help us to agree on the basic and common business definition. For example, when working with a product, what is the product hierarchy used (if more are available)? How will some measures be calculated (YTD, MTD, comparison of the actual and the plan…)? Or what security will be applied – will every user see everything? Alternatively, dedicated users from different regions could see just the data for the region, or users from the region could see detailed data for their region but aggregated data for the rest? In general, we can find at least the following areas that need to be agreed upon from the business perspective

— Data Security concepts
— KPI definitions
— Dimension's definition
— Visualization patterns – if there are any

Ensure technical development standards

As it could happen that more technical squads are working on the report's development, we need to ensure the consistency of such development across the squads. That could help us with both economies of scale (as we can create reusable patterns within the delivery that are project-specific; for example, how to calculate YTD changes for any metrics) and flexibility (in case we need to move a team member across the squads or create a new squad). Some time needs to be dedicated to sharing best practices and managing the technical debt during the implementation – or ideally, technical debt creation should be minimised by following standards from the beginning. If you think about it, this could be done by a centralized function/squad.

Produce the report itself

This is a critical part of the technical work – report development. As you can see, in an ideal world, the two previous steps should be clarified in advance; otherwise, these squads will not be working fully effectively. We are looking at the effectiveness of the overall project, which leads us to a different approach. The squads are iterating with stakeholders above prototypes (MVPs – minimal valuable products). And these prototypes help to define standards (both technical and business ones).

As you can see, the critical aspect here is balance – mastering the relation between centralized functions (business and technical standards) and the speed of development. At the beginning of the project, we need to ensure we have at least basic standards to avoid significant redesigns (which could mean that many tough decisions will need to happen). The most important part of the project is communication – it needs to be transparent and effective. Technical debt created during the project needs to be perceived as a good thing – as it helps define the standards. Also, space must be dedicated to addressing technical debt – so at some point, work on the technical debt will need to be prioritized.

As we now understand the tasks to be done and the workflow, let us look at how to structure a team. There could be many options as the team's formal boundaries could be overcome by good communication. For example, you can have a central business team, central best practices team and delivery squads. Or you can distribute business people into delivery squads to ensure good alignment with business features. There probably is no one right way – a lot depends on the concrete project itself and company structure. However, organizing the team in a certain way could increase risks in some areas (if we do not have a centralized technical team, we increase the risk of technical inconsistency within the delivery squads). So, it is more about setting up teams to ensure all three main tasks and implement a system of communication (for example, supported by metrics) that will help limit the risk.

Let us just show one example that we would consider as working in most cases. A central business team could be established to define basic business concepts and explain the impact to stakeholders. The technical standard competency (ensuring technical standards) could be distributed in the delivery squads (teams delivering reports) as the people from these teams could help with the delivery and should teach tech developers directly during the work. Two main communication channels need to be established and followed. First, technical leads synchronize regularly and share breaches of best practices or new project-specific patterns. Second, intensive communication with business needs to happen – as the business team needs to have immediate feedback on what a business decision means from a technical standpoint. They need to provide answers to any questions asked by the delivery squad quickly. We have tried to visualize the following set-up in Figure 3.5 (Data processing is in the chart, but just for an illustrative reason – as it is addressed externally):

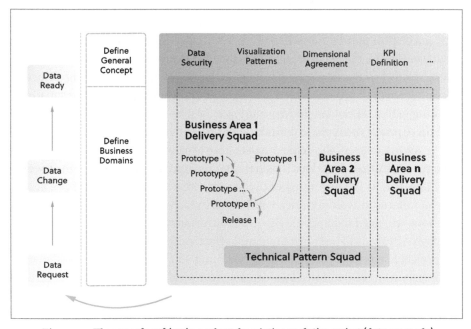

Figure 3.5: The way of working in a robust descriptive analytics project (data are ready)

A small-scale project could be delivered with considerably easier concepts. If enough technical people know the business, it could be straightforward (the most prominent problem might be IT standards that need to be followed to deploy into the production). The scale is impacted by the complexity of the business area and the number of stakeholders that need to agree.

3.2.3   WoW – Robust descriptive analytics project (data are not ready)

This type of analytics is, from some perspectives, very similar to the previous one – there is just one significant difference. Data preparation is part of the project. It means that part of the project is creating a centralized data storage (in any form) that has value to stakeholders (without reporting). It could look like a small change, but it is significant for many reasons – from expectation management to the toolset needed for the WoW.

First, we can see this as an analytics solution (composed of two projects, data preparation and data visualization). However, this approach will not help us from the project management perspective (organizing the WoW) – instead of having one project that is quite complex, we have two with less complexity but higher dependency. The work that needs to be done is still the same. From that perspective, it could be better to include this within one project, as the coordination should be easier (and the management overhead as well).

As you can imagine, the biggest problem in such a project is to synchronize the data preparation and reporting stream. Both have different principles and different assumptions that need to be considered. In the previous chapter (3.2.2 WoW – Robust descriptive analytics project (data are ready)), we have described the pure reporting "stream" approach in quite some detail. The same approach can be used for the reporting part in this type of project as well. The only difference is that further synchronization needs to happen with the "data preparation team". Like before, this can be solved in two different ways – we can embed people with the data knowledge into the reporting squads, or we need to ensure extensive communication between reporting and data preparation teams. As the data preparation team needs to work closely together for many reasons (we will look at them later), it may be better to have an independent data team with intensive communication with reporting squads. So, the WoW for reporting squads could be visualized in Figure 3.6.

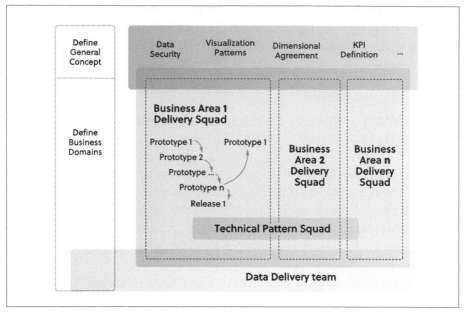

Figure 3.6: The way of working in a robust descriptive analytics project (data are not ready)

To summarize the approach, we have a business team and a data team set up as separate units (squads), but the reporting best practice team is directly embedded into the reporting squads.

Let us look at how the data delivery team could cooperate with the other one in general. As there are two other teams in the system, two main types of communication need to happen. Cooperation with the business team is mainly focused on the data sources (which data to use), data ownership (who owns and describes the data), and data calculation (that should happen as part of the data preparation). From one perspective, the cooperation has the same scope as between the reporting and business teams in the previous example (3.2.2 WoW – Robust descriptive analytics project (data are ready)). However, the expectation management needs to be different:

— There could be a significant dependency on the DWH company strategy
    — What kind of data modelling delivery approach
      is used (Centralized or Federated)?
    — What kind of DWH is used – Inmon, Kimbal, Data Vault...?
— There is not much flexibility; changes take time to implement
    — Changing one data source for another could take time
    — Negotiating even to start ingesting data could take a time
— Some dependencies are difficult to overcome
    — You cannot start data modelling before you see
      the data (or you can but with some risk)

Limited flexibility, strictly defined standards, and dependencies could lead to a waterfall way of thinking – and it is valid from some perspectives. In this case, the agile way of working is more in line with the culture of delivery. The teams need to be ready to prototype or jump from task to task. Individual team members also need to be prepared to work in different areas of the data preparation stream. Let us have a look at the following visualization:

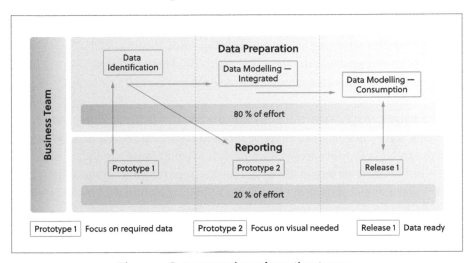

Figure 3.7: Data preparation and reporting streams –
dependencies and different rhythms of the work

Figure 3.7 shows that the data preparation stream contains more phases that you need to pass through, and it is quite impossible to skip one (data identification/ ingest → data modelling → consumption). This dependency (flow) is the waterfall component of the delivery. The technology set used for data modelling depends on the enterprise standard, but, commonly, one person can do each step on the data journey covered by the Data Preparation team. More precisely, experts are needed, but in general, it is still possible to have them in one squad and leverage this collocation, as experts usually can cover multiple areas (and they are used to it). The challenge could lie in the cooperation with the business team – as the people in the data team are usually very technically focused, we need to have people who would like to understand data from a business perspective and are ready to talk with business people to discuss the business meaning. Vice versa, the business team needs to be ready to answer tough questions around the data, as every business logic needs to be described in a general way (otherwise, it is not possible to implement it). Most of the work could be hidden in the business understanding of the data, which is later reflected in the data transformation and modelling (security…).

Cooperation with the reporting team is more challenging – as this part needs to reflect a different way of delivery (quick prototyping in the reporting team versus less flexible and dependent delivery in the data team). As you can see from Figure 3.7, the reporting team could do the prototyping based on the data on a different level (meaning on a different level of the data journey in the project itself – identification, integrated, consumption). The ideal situation is to go through the following steps:

1.   The reporting team could help to identify the data
      needed – by visualizing them for end-users.
2.   The reporting team could help to identify ideal data structures
      needed for reporting by using a prototype visualization.
3.   Technical experts in the reporting team could help to create
      consolidated data requirements from different reporting streams.

The challenge is to synchronize the rhythm of work of both the data preparation and reporting teams. Namely, prototyping speed in reporting areas is usually quicker than the speed in the data preparation part. This could cause significant technical debt – just because we would like to release the report (put it into production) as quickly as possible. Let us have a look at the following picture with more details:

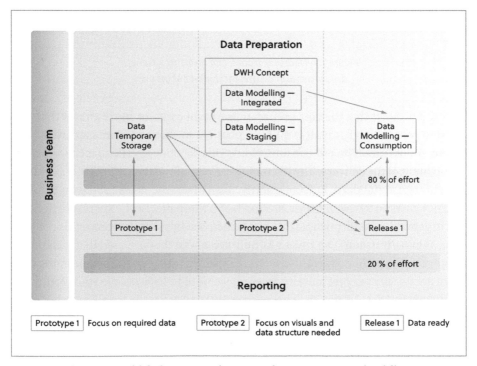

Figure 3.8: Multiple data preparation approaches to support reporting delivery

In Figure 3.8 you can see that "Prototype 2" (and the same for "Release 1") could be done using many sources of data:

1. Directly from the Data Source (Data Temporary Storage) – if it is urgent to visualize data directly in the data source, to identify the right one
2. Data Staging
3. Data Integrated Model
4. Data Consumption Layer

This possibility will bring agility into the delivery ecosystem. On the other hand, it also brings the technical debt that needs to be addressed later. If we add the possibility of releasing the report (put it into production, see box "Release 1") from different data layers, we will potentially open the door to a problem with stakeholder expectations. As soon as the report is deployed, it could be challenging to find a reason (time and money) to reconnect it to the correct data source (the data consumption layer) as there is no significant benefit for the end-user (which could mean that other tasks with a more tangible business value will be prioritized).

3.2.4 WoW – Analytics ecosystem (including AA)

As you can imagine, adding the advanced analytics squad into the general picture is the most complex setup that could exist. In such a case, the advanced analytics team usually works in two modes: Experimentation and Industrialization.

In Experimentation, the approach is the same as in the first use case (3.2.1 WoW - Advanced analytics ad-hoc project). The team can leverage any data from any data source (within and outside of the project scope). Only if the algorithm is industrialized (make a robust solution from experimentation) will the team move to the second mode of cooperation. Unfortunately, that does not always happen due to the following reasons (we have already mentioned this, so just a reminder):

— The advanced analytics algorithm did not work
— It does not make sense to industrialize the advanced analytics algorithm, as it only tackles a one-time problem
— The advanced analytics algorithm is too expensive to industrialize

In Industrialization, the advanced analytics team behaves basically the same as the reporting team – just using a different toolset (sometimes, both visualization and advanced analytics work could be done in one tool). Therefore, they help identify the data needed and provide feedback on the data structure required. They can have the same challenge with data consumption and deployment as the reporting team (creation of technical debt). However, there are two main differences. First, the advanced analytics team also generates new data (forecasts, for example). We need to see the advanced analytics component as another data source that needs to be integrated into the data ecosystem. Second, the advanced analytics team has less experience with industrialization activities, meaning this step might be underestimated (this is because projects in this area tend to be less industrialized in general – see the chapter about typical projects).

As the overview of such a project is quite complex, you can see a visualization (Figure 3.9) that is on a higher level than the previous ones.

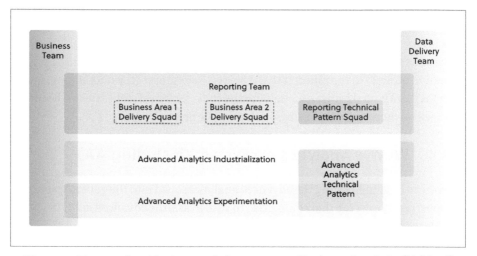

Figure 3.9: The way of working in an analytics ecosystem with advanced analytics (high level)

Small-scale projects are the hardest to find in this area. It is unique that one person would have the experiences with all the aspects of such work, making the team structure less complicated.

The biggest question is the company's data strategy and concept and the processes connected with adding new data or analytical applications into the company data ecosystem. Usually, at least some data integration within a separate analytical application is the preferred way to implement additional insight. There could be workarounds (both technical and business-wise) for skipping the required data integration (which could be on many different levels), which usually significantly decreases the work complexity. Reducing this complexity leads to quicker implementation, which manifests primarily in lower costs and faster business outcomes. Secondarily, it decreases the risk of wasted work. If we follow such an approach, the division of effort is not valid anymore (the 80 to 20 ratio mentioned in Figure 3.7). If we do so, we need to recognise that from the overall company perspective, new technology debt is created as the project builds new data silos – maybe we can name it "data debt", but it is usually included in the technical debt category. What has greater business benefits should be carefully assessed – the speed of the delivery or integrated data. The same goes for the technology stack

– some tools could be used for the overall project, but only on some scale. So, for a single project, it may be beneficial to try that, but the limits could likely be reached later – for example, in the number of transformations, performance, security... We need to understand the impact on every category in the IT landscape. Again, it is possible to create significant technical debt if we want to grow in the future (from an analytical perspective).

3.2.5   WoW – Summary

As you can see, the WoW could be very complex and could differ significantly with each type of analytics. However, it is not easy to define the best WoW, even for a single type of analytics, as it depends not only on all three axes of the system but also on the team experience and the company/team delivery culture. What works for one project/team does not necessarily have to work for another one. Ultimately, the project is a set of individuals who should support each other. And if the team finds a way to do it, it is not as important how it is formalized. However, we hope that we provided at least a high-level idea of how to organize the work.

We need to realize that the methodology used for delivery (in the extreme definitions of waterfall and agile) will not solve the delivery problem. What will help us establish the working ecosystem is understanding the flow of the work (and data) in the system together with understanding flexibility in every step. That, together with the correct methodology, could lead to successful project implementation.

There is obviously always a business team in any analytical type of analytics described above. Involving the business team (and their active participation) is critical for the project's success. This is well-known advice, but it is so essential that it makes sense to repeat it one more time.

The last comment – the WoW can change with the project life cycle. There could be many reasons – it could be because the system is established, because more data are available, different analytical tasks are needed, or just because different teams now know how to work together. So, what we need to do is constantly monitor the WoW. And we need to leverage the results of monitoring to improve systems if required.

3.3   Industrialization challenge

The industrialization challenge is about managing stakeholder expectations and understanding the complexity of work in different stages of the solution. Specifically, we can see this when moving from the ad-hoc to the robust solution. However, as mentioned in the chapter 3.2 Ways of working - WoW, an element of experimentation or prototyping is also included in robust projects. Typical questions connected with this challenge are the following:

1. Why is industrialization taking so long (why it is so expensive)?
2. Why did the project team not develop it properly from the beginning?
3. Why do we even need to do industrialization?

Let us try to have a look at these questions in more detail. It is important to realize that we need to provide business answers (ideally), as these questions are valid. The common reasoning over IT standards that need to be followed could initiate a discussion around the quality of standards in general (are the standards set up right if meeting them is so expensive?) and therefore it could have a negative impact on the project delivery (from a certain perspective, we will reduce the maturity on the IT landscape axis). Just to emphasise, we are not saying that every IT standard is right and well-defined (mainly due to the current dynamic in the technology available on the market). Again, it is about finding the balance between the flexibility that can speed up development and standards as a reusable, proven and secure pattern – but defining IT standards is not within the scope of this book. We need to realise that if we want to shift the defined standards within the project, it will introduce further complexity into the delivery (and move us into a different area then analytics project implementation).

3.3.1   Why is the industrialization taking so long?

That is s very fair question to ask. We hope that we provided enough reasoning and examples for the complexity associated with the industrialization process across the three axes (and the resulting costs) in the three-axis approach. In the context of managing stakeholder expectations, we believe that in this case, we should change their mindset and try to reformulate it – change the focus from costs to benefits. So, the right question is what we gain from industrialization – and there could be great deal.

IT perspective

From an IT perspective, we can gain regular support and some already developed patterns that we can use. Usually, these are not very visible, but we need to highlight them. It should be much cheaper to use an already established environment than develop a new one (think, for example, about the licenses). It should be scalable from a performance perspective, and it should be much more secure from an enterprise perspective. So, the extra money that we expend because of following standards (which may not necessarily be as flexible as we need) should return easily due to synergies with different projects. In general, there are two problematic areas. First, it is not necessarily visible at the beginning of the project (when it could be even the other way around), but the longer the project will run (the more robust analytics ecosystem will be created), the more payback we gain. Managing this time shift exactly could be challenging. Second, the economy of scale could be valid across multiple projects – so the costs for the company overall could be lower if five projects take the same approach (standards, environments). However, this does not necessarily mean, that every single project will have lower expenses. There could be some projects that are simply more expensive (but others are much cheaper). It this case, we speak about managing expectations on the company level (which bring us back to the analytics maturity axis – company analytics maturity).

Business perspective

While the IT perspective is about technology, the business perspective is mainly about data. Having data in one place could be valuable (we are not saying that the only option is to store them in one database scheme). The next project (release) could easily leverage what was already done and be much quicker. In this case, we are not talking only about the data itself, but about the reports, advanced analytics models, Metadata descriptions, and report catalogues. It could go even further to include areas like access management or enterprise search. As you can imagine, everyone would see the benefits there, but unfortunately, not everyone understands that it also means that certain standards need to be followed during the implementation. It could be an extra task (money and time) that is not directly required by the project (like data description), but it will bring benefits for other analytical questions (moving us ahead on the analytics axis – we would be more ready for another step). We can also say that increasing Data Maturity is beneficial for the company but could be expensive for one project.

Moreover, we will gain scalability and robustness of the solution – which should decrease several types of risk. For example, security should be done correctly, or the risk of solution outages should decrease as well.

3.3.2   Why is it not robust from the beginning?

Again, this is a very valid question – we need to understand that we are trying to balance the speed of the prototyping and following development standards within the robust solution. We need to try to bring these two extremes as close together as possible – this will help us save time for industrialization by limiting redevelopment. However, if we follow all the standards from the beginning, the prototyping phase does not make sense – as everything is developed so that it is ready to be deployed in the production. It could be very visible for the advanced analytics stream. If the squad waits for a regular load of data before they start experimentation, they will not have the flexibility needed. Additionally, it could easily happen that the analytical approach will turn out to be wrong, which will automatically mean that data are not needed at all (in an extreme case).

Do not take us wrong – we believe that reducing the time and effort needed to move from prototyping to robust solution is critical for a successful project. Anything that can be done to improve this area will be repaid quickly. However, it will always be about the right balance – and this balance needs to be explained to stakeholders.

Looking for the right balance between value today and value tomorrow is well aligned with agile concepts like the Minimum Viable Product and continuous iterations on improving such a product. But if we take a more ad-hoc approach in some areas, stakeholders might be surprised that improving the product and industrialization requires changes that they thought had already been made. This can slow down activities that are considered valuable by the stakeholders making the project team look unprofessional ("why didn't they implement such basic things at the beginning?"). Therefore, we must constantly evaluate the complexities described in the three-axis approach and manage stakeholder expectations.

Continuous improvement and continuous development have become a trend in the last year and could be considered the right way to limit the impact of this challenge. It could help speed up the development from the beginning and move to a robust solution. However, the specifics of the analytics project need to be considered, especially because data are the goal (not a feature). For example, the development of automatic testing for every single possible data combination could be challenging (or even not possible). So, such a task could be a long ongoing process into which we need to invest.

3.3.3   Why do we even need to do industrialization?

The answer should already be clear from the two questions above – it is because standardization brings benefits. It is more about comparing short-term and long-term investment/profitability. That is exactly why proper stakeholder management is needed as the money invested is in the stakeholders' hands.

Just to emphasize once more – the willingness to spend money on industrialization (when it makes sense) could be considered part of the company analytics maturity (company maturity).

3.4   Time impact

We have already discussed the three axes that are critically important for analytics projects. We have also described commonalities of analytics projects and highlighted why they are important. In the next section, we would like to quickly look at another aspect – how the project develops over time. Until now, we have been looking at the project at specific points in time. But is the approach (project categorization) consistent as the project moves ahead, with time running?

The answer is very easy – it is not. Like everything else, the project evolves, so the analytical need evolves as well. But as you can imagine, the development in time could impact the position on all three axes, and even the commonalities could be changing...

3.4.1   Regular re-evaluation of the three axes as a continuous process

Re-evaluation of the position on the three axes needs to be done regularly. Or maybe, it needs to be done continuously, and we need to understand the dynamics in every category.

Analytics Maturity

In an ideal situation, we should be moving forward on the analytics journey (from descriptive to cognitive). We should move step by step as the analytics project never ends. However, this is not the only direction that a project could take to shift in the analytics maturity model:

— We can move from an ad-hoc to a robust solution (automation is needed)
— We can move on the analytics journey (descriptive to predictive)
— We can scale up an existing solution by adding additional insight based on existing data (creating another report)

The change (shift) of the scope could be (and usually is) gradual, meaning that it could be easily missed. Slow changes in the scope of regular tasks could be a good indicator that something is happening. For example, we can see:

— An increase of prototyping/experimentation tasks
— A rise in technical tasks focusing on automation
— Tasks focusing on defining new metrics and expanding the report

Moreover, stakeholder maturity could change – in both directions. If the project is successful and brings the desired results, the stakeholders' risk appetite could increase and make them want to try new areas and implement the insight generated by analytical methods in different business areas. Additionally, stakeholders learn, and they may have more realistic expectations about what can be delivered. However, it could be the other way around – if the project is slow and does not meet their expectation, there could be pressure to invest in the analytical approach somewhere else. The same is valid for company maturity. The time delay can be greater as the communication needs more time, but on the other hand, company maturity is influenced by other projects as well – so the change there could be unexpected and completely out of our control. Again, it could be influenced by a change in the market (for example, events like data leaks or the ethical problems of Artificial Intelligence). We also need to realize that the value generated by projects will vary over time – for many reasons (for example, adding further insight or including more users). This means that the stakeholder group could evolve as well.

Data Maturity

As analytics maturity evolves, data maturity could evolve as well. Again, both positive and negative development is possible.

The first situation could be that the project requires more data. Bringing additional data sources is always a complication, primarily due to integration challenges. If we did not expect the integration with an additional data source, we could have considerable trouble including the data source into the existing data model (not to mention standard integration issues). Imagine that at the beginning, you need to deliver analysis for one country only (and you did not plan for the possibility that additional countries could be added). In such a case, you can limit the data structures and data processes to this assumption. It could mean that you are not using the country code within your tables or did not consider the currency and conversion rate a vital concept that needs to be implemented in the data flow from the beginning. It could mean that you need to redesign the overall solution. And redesigning the solution means that you need to revise what you have already deployed into production.

Other examples that could bring the same challenges could be:

— More granular data needed
— More complex security requirements
    (as we included more countries, for example)
— More groups of users with a different security model

The requirements above may move us to the left on the Data Maturity axis (Low).

Let us look at the opposite situation – when we prepare for the potential integration well (for example, we define a flexible security model), we can leverage it for a new data source. From that perspective, it could move us ahead on the Data Maturity axis as we become more ready to absorb new data sets quickly.

A specific situation could be when another project would like to leverage the data set you have created. In such a case, you take on the role of the data provider, and one of the project benefits could move from "generating insight directly to consumers" to being a "provider of consolidated data". As you can imagine, this change has a significant impact on the WoW and stakeholder management (it is realistic to presume that stakeholders do not want to be in the role of data providers at all).

IT Maturity

Both changes in analytics maturity and data maturity could significantly influence the IT landscape. Different analytical tasks could mean that other IT tools need to be added to the ecosystem. Unfortunately, more complex tasks (more data, complex security models) could influence the initial selection of the tool (that we potentially made properly in the past). Such a situation could mean technical reimplementation of the solution (could generate significant technical debt). Managing the situation in which you need to resolve the technical debt and deliver new business functionality could make the delivery model extremely complex, with a high cost increase for some time.

Basically, the movement in the three-axis box could go in every direction. Ideally, we want to move toward higher IT maturity, data maturity and analytics maturity. However, even this is not necessarily true:

—   We can find that some types of analytics do not make sense –
      we can give up the cognitive approach, for example. This will
      decrease our analytics maturity from some points of view.
—   As we will be trying to include new data, data maturity could
      decrease due to the new data source characteristics.
—   As we hit the boundaries of the IT environment (for example, because
      we need to include unstructured data), the overall IT maturity
      could decrease as well (or IT maturity for the next increment).

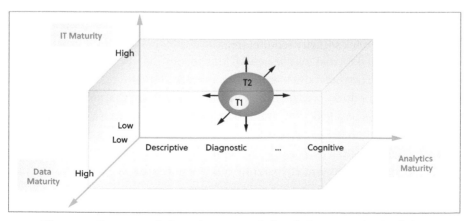

Figure 3.10: From an analytics project to an analytics solution – example of evolution

If the project is successful, we could see the change from project to solution (more analytics disciplines covered within the project). In such a case, it is crucial to identify this trend early on and change the WoW on the project (together with stakeholder management). You can see the basic visualisation in Figure 3.10 (T1 means time 1 and T2 is time 2).

Finally, let us provide two extreme examples that could demonstrate a situation in which a project does not assess the change of time and follows the original delivery concept.

Never-ending MVP (Minimal Valuable Product)

This could be typical for a project that started as rapid prototyping or even experimentation. The MVP was released to end-users; they liked it and defined the next version. As business tasks are always prioritized, the solution moves quickly from the business value perspective, but it could generate a great deal of technical debt. For example, it could be represented by the delivery team providing support or incorrect use of the IT landscape (using the ad-hoc environment for a robust solution). In this case, it had not been correctly re-evaluated that the project had moved from the prototyping phase to a regular analytics solution. Usually, every single increment of MVP increases the problem – so it is more complicated to change the mindset. This situation could happen when business stakeholders mainly drive the project.

The solution there is straightforward (at least to write; it could be challenging to do). We need to evaluate the project regularly and have good and open communication with stakeholders from the beginning.

Never-ending "industrialization"

This is the opposite situation, which is sometimes defined as "doing IT for IT". In such a case, before the business value is delivered (for example, visualization), there is a great deal of focus on the solution robustness (preparation of the environment or preparation of data that may be needed for the solution). Still, it could be a valid strategy – but we need to move to a different approach (creating the business value) later. If we do not do so, we will have a very robust system that nobody is using. There can always be a task that could increase the IT robustness. This situation could happen when the IT department is strong and can significantly influence the project. An essential part of an analytics project is regularly collecting feedback from real users – and it could help us find out when we are heading into a situation like that described above.

To summarize – managing an analytics project properly over time is magic. It is mainly about balance: Is it better to generate technical debt for potential future development or delay the first release by doing complex analysis of possible future problems? This is precisely the situation in which you need to have a very good overview of all the analytics disciplines (not just a siloed view – we discussed that at the very beginning of the book, in the "Analytics project paradox"). What can help is open communication and a long-term implementation strategy that includes a plan for potential future development (shift) on any axes. To ensure that we know in which stage of the project we are, we need to monitor the development continually and evaluate the shift on all axes. And if the change happens, it is necessary to leverage the prepared strategy in time.

3.4.2   Product Life Cycle management

We will not discuss Product Life Cycle management as this topic would need a dedicated book of its own. However, let us look at some ideas that could help us understand this area in connection with the previous chapters.

The development described in the previous chapter (3.4.1 Regular re-evaluation of the three axes as a continuous process) has an impact on the general scope of the project. However, we also need to understand what to do with the previously implemented parts of the solution because the new scope does not only mean new development; we also need to address how we will maintain the already developed (even deployed) parts of the solution. Creating new assets could significantly change the balance of work that needs to happen. Simply put, at the beginning of the project, it is about the new development. Later, it could be about the maintenance of existing solutions. The more we have deployed, the more maintenance work will need to be done. Sometimes, it is done by different departments; sometimes, it is managed by the project team – this may also evolve. We briefly discussed the support models in the chapters 1.3.4 Are processes established? and 2.5 Maintenance of analytics.

This could have a couple of significant effects. First, the delivery team may potentially need to be changed. We may need different types of people. There could be a shift from wildly creative people looking for new ways to do work to more process-oriented people with a focus on the automation and management of complex solutions. If we do not realize it soon enough, we risk that some people will even leave the project (company). We also need to understand that these two different groups of people have the same importance for the analytics ecosystem – one cannot effectively exist without the other.

Second, the funding model needs to change. The funding needs will probably grow (if we are still doing new development). We need to expect that there will be pushback, and we will need to look for ways to leverage the economies of scale (once again, another reason why process-oriented people will be crucial for us in later phases of the project). Moreover, the business case for the solution needs to be built differently – we can start slowly moving from the generation of new insight into maintaining the insight provided. And you can see that different calculations of rentability of investment need to be done for these two different scenarios.

Third, stakeholder management needs to change based on the two categories mentioned above. There is a new motivation for stakeholders to invest in the solution, leading to stakeholder change. The shift from one stakeholder to another is not always easy and could have a major impact on the delivery team.

3.4.3   External factors

There are still many external events that could dramatically affect us, and we cannot control them at all.

One of them is the IT evolution. Developments in the IT landscape are rapid and tough to follow. Most of us are overwhelmed by marketing materials from many companies promising quick results. Usually, these are visible in three main areas:

— A completely different concept of analytics project delivery
— A shift from technical to business-driven development
(you need to have less technical expertise for development, which means that business people can do it)
— A technological "revolution" – a new technology that could shift the speed of development/calculation or the volume of the data to another level

It is good (or even crucial) to follow up on these developments and constantly evaluate our IT landscape compared to the market IT landscape. We do not want to discuss how to do it in this book or when it makes sense to invest in a new toolset and reimplement (although such a new trend could be easily misused). However, if you think about the content of this book, it is not technologically focused. We believe that you still need to consider every aspect mentioned in this book – but the results may differ based on the technology landscape available (in many aspects – from the delivery team composition to the tool selection and the support model leveraged). Also, remember that including a new tool in the analytics ecosystem is an IT project, not an analytics project. Hence, a different approach may be needed.

Another one is market (industry) development. There could be many events that slow down/speed up the investment into analytics solutions.

First, it depends on the industry economic period. If the industry grows, investments will likely be higher (as any new investment needs money). Even though some projects may be focused on cost-effectiveness, investment is still necessary.

Second, it could be any event on the market that influences the overall trust in analytics. Any risk event associated with bad insight could have both positive and negative impacts on the situation in a specific company. Either it could lead to a higher level of investment as the market could force the company to provide more insight into some area (it could even be due to regulation), or it could halt the investment into some areas as there was a negative case connected with a similar analysis on the market.

It is probably impossible to influence it, but we can at least try to be ready.

3.4.4   Vendor lock-in

There is also another situation that could still influence us from a long-term perspective and that may not be particularly visible at the beginning of the project or can significantly change its position later. This is known as vendor lock-in. Vendor lock-in is a situation in which a customer using a product(s), service(s) or resource(s) cannot easily transition to a competitor's product(s), service(s), or resource(s). This may mean not just another company whose products, services or resources would benefit us, but competitors can also refer to the company's internal products, services, or resources.

In the essence of vendor lock-in types, we can focus on potential risks and failures from the IT maturity, analytics maturity, and data maturity perspectives:

IT Maturity

We are using the components, tools, or services of one vendor or a consortium of vendors. We can be happy as we think we are using the best the market offers for our work, we can operate without any major issues and comply with the company architecture and technology stack. This will obviously work for ad-hoc initiatives without any problem. For robust initiatives and industrialization, we may deal more with company architecture and strategy, license costs and policy, or integration with other systems and platforms. Technologies are usually proprietary without much (if any) compatibility with competitors, and migration from one component, tool, or service to another can be challenging, time-consuming, and costly.

In many cases, migration such as this may cause significant refactoring of almost the whole solution if the maturity of our technology and platform is not on a sufficient level, developed using the latest widely used frameworks and best practices that can reduce refactoring needs and are de facto open for cooperation across the IT landscape. We must emphasise that we still see many products and services that are not open to such cooperation in the analytics field. If we get into an IT vendor lock-in, various issues will be added to our plate if the IT landscape needs to be changed for any reason. It could be worth considering following standards that would allow easier migration to other technology (for example, not to use vendor-specific functions). On the other hand, this approach will slow down development and decrease the technical value of the tool we decided to use.

Analytics Maturity

Next to technology vendor lock-in, we can also encounter a resources and services vendor lock-in: analytics maturity vendor lock-in. Typically, we outsource the work to an external team (one or more persons) with stronger privileges for communicating with business and other involved teams. Although we check with our external delivery team progress regularly, we can simply miss some core parts of the solution or some communication with business and other teams. The external delivery team becomes more advanced and skilled in the business domain, develops trust with all parties, and it is easier for us to involve the same team in other development activities again and again. The main risk arising from this situation is that knowledge revolves around delivery. We can have a "black-box" solution that we only understand very little from the business point of view (besides the technology). Mitigation approaches can include having internal analysts closely work with the external team, establishing regular reviews of not just analytics outcomes but also reviews of methodology and the steps that lead to the outcomes, and setting standards for thorough documentation of methodology and requiring them.

Data Maturity

Similarly to analytics maturity, the "black-box" solution can also occur in the data area if we rely too much on an external party in data integration and data engineering work. The mitigation approach here is similar to that for analytics maturity. Another risk is if we are overly dependent on external data from one specific vendor. To mitigate vendor lock-in in this area, it might be wise to review existing data provisioning contracts, see if there are alternative providers of similar data sets on the market or see to what extent we can achieve our analytical objectives with our internal data.

The vendor lock-in situation is riskier for robust and long-term initiatives. For ad-hoc, we can benefit from it if we do not plan industrialization. In that case, vendor lock-in probability should be mitigated as much as possible. For smaller companies and companies with lower IT and analytics maturity, a well-managed potential vendor lock-in can also be a benefit in terms of speedy delivery of all parts of the solution.

A similar lock-in situation can happen for internal resources as well, e.g., for a resource that is too experienced and unique, and we do not consider any backup or proper knowledge sharing (documentation) within the company.

It is indubitable that vendor lock-in has an impact not only on time but also on costs, risks, and basically the whole delivery of our analytics initiative. So, plan your analytical initiatives to emphasise not falling into vendor lock-ins and make a backup plan to ensure situations like this are resolved effectively without significant impact.

The analytics project generates value by providing insight from the data. It includes the understanding of the process of how insight is generated. Otherwise, we are creating an external system that provides insight. Basically, we are buying insight instead of generating it. As mentioned, this could be perfectly okay, but it is not recommended for critical business processes or applications.

4 Typical failures and risks per project types

To provide a more tangible point of view, we would like to look at things from the opposite angle. So far, we have been looking at the typical characteristics of the analytics project (and how to categorise them). We will look at specific types of projects, provide a high-level assessment of their characteristics from a risk perspective (highly generalised), and comment on the most common problems or challenges.

It is no easy task. There are so many assumptions that need to be considered to set up the surrounding environment for the project, which could significantly influence the evaluation. Let us show just one example – the size of the company.

For small companies (for example, up to 30 people), it is less probable that there will be a dedicated team of data science people. A reporting tool may not necessarily be available. For massive companies (more than 1000 people), we can be sure that at least some data science people are scattered around, and a reporting tool should be ready as well. It is impossible to compare the same project (project type) across these two companies from that perspective. The same could be the case across different industries or even regions.

Despite that fact, we have tried to highlight the most significant risks that we commonly see for specific project categorization. Please take them only as an example – they could help you evaluate whether you are in the same situation. Of course, the real risks could lie elsewhere, so you need to do your evaluation correctly (even for categories that we did not identify as risky).

For every concrete project type, we evaluate the risks independently. We are trying to highlight the most significant challenges that could come up without any comparison with other types of projects. For example, there could be high risk in a specific area for one project type and a medium risk in the same area for another project type. However, this does not say anything about the comparison of this risk within two project types. You always need to look at it only from the perspective of one project. There could be specific chapters focusing on the comparison, but these are always highlighted and include an explicit mention in the chapter description.

4.1 Advanced analytics projects – Ad-hoc (Predictive)

Table 4.1 shows the evaluation of the risks, challenges, and commonalities for Advanced Analytics projects – Ad-hoc.

		Risk rate	Comments
Three-Axis Approach			
Analytics Maturity	Stakeholder Maturity	Low	**A**
	Company Analytics Maturity	Low	**A**
	Analytics Landscape Maturity	Low	**A**
	Market	Low	**A**
Data Maturity	Are data available	Medium	**B**
	Are data integrated	Low	
	Are data described	Medium	**B**
	Is data security clear	Low	**C**
IT Maturity	Are tools available	Low	
	Are tools integrated	Low	
	Are tools flexible	Low	**D**
	Are processes established		
	Access to Toolset	Medium	**D**
	Best Practices	Low	
	Deployment Standards	Low	
	Support Models	Low	
	Delivery Model	Low	
Common Attributes			
Agile x Waterfall		Low	
Data-driven		Low	
Technology Mix		Low	
Data Oriented Thinking		Low	
Maintenance of Analytics		NA	
Prototyping and Experimentation		Low	
Challenges			
Management Expectations		Medium	**E**
WoW		Low	
Industrialization Challenge		Low (Medium)	**E**
Time Impact			
Time Impact		Low	**E**

Table 4.1: Risk evaluation for typical ad-hoc advanced analytics projects (predictive)

A Predictive analysis is the first step going beyond reporting on the analytics journey. This is an already known discipline with many implementations across industries. From that perspective, there is no significant risk in this category. Still, we need to be aware of the challenges that could happen (described in the chapter 1.1 Axis 1: Analytics Maturity) when they are connected to accepting analytics results without having complete insight into the mechanics of the calculation.

B If there is a trigger for a new predictive analytics ad-hoc project, the required source data are typically identified and available. But we should watch out for the data quality (if the data have not yet been used for this type of analytics) and data description (see the data maturity section). Additionally, we should check if enough data have been collected – e.g., we might need at least 36 months of historical data to get reasonable precision of the forecasting model, but the system has only been storing data for 24 months. In such an example, even with good data quality, the limited history of the data can make it challenging to reach the algorithms' desired accuracy.

C In such a case, data security is not usually a problem. It could be solved easily as usually only one person (or a limited number of people) has access to the detailed data. For example, a Non-Disclosure Agreement could be signed with the delivery team. The result is usually on an aggregated level (although data could be very granular). That means there are usually no security issues with sharing the results (with the relevant audience). However, from some perspectives, this generates technical debt for potential future "next steps".

D The toolset itself is not problematic – plenty of open-source tools could help. The problem could be the potential limitation on the company side (for example, the end-user is not authorized to install R on the computer). More commonly, the person is authorized to install, but it takes time. The time required for installation (access to the tool) might be longer than the time needed for the analysis itself. This challenge could relate to the toolset flexibility. As we are trying to prove something new, it is often done in new ways (a new type of analytical method needs to be applied, new visualisation of data is required). There could be an IT toolset available for such an experimentation approach. But it could easily happen that the tools established in the company lack an out-of-the-box capability. This situation usually causes the tendency to use new tools that immediately have the desired feature (without any review of the potential future impact). Furthermore, there could be a tendency to use the tool you are used to (even though the established tool has the same capability). All this could cause a potential future challenge with industrialization (we have discussed this throughout the book, for example, in the chapters 3.3 Industrialization challenge or 1.4 Ad-hoc x Robust – amplification).

E Depending on the overall analytics maturity, predictive analytics can be matured well, with some validated technology stack and processes. One could say that the solution is like a descriptive type of analytics with models in advance. And it is an ad-hoc solution, with all the characteristics of ad-hoc projects, to be used ideally only once or with a limited execution with defined (hardcoded) inputs (of course, assuming there are no good reasons for a robust project from the beginning). Management overwhelmed by interesting results usually forgets this fact and simply asks for the same execution on a new data set with new parameters again and again. That is possible, but after a few iterations, it is a good time to think about industrialization. Industrialization will not only represent building deployment; in many cases, it will cause significant code refactoring. All hardcoded variables must be parametrized or pulled by data in an automated way, not to mention the environment, so that the next execution period can be affected. Moreover, all this applies to situations where the model performs well.

For the industrialization challenges that this type of project brings, it is good to stop at the beginning of the project or after its first iterations, look back at how the solution has been implemented so far, and review the business purpose of the solution and its use in the future. Based on this discussion, we should recognize whether we can continue with the ad-hoc approach, or we should invest in a robust solution and prepare for industrialization at some point. The delivery curve can be flattened, and we can get worse burndown, but it is probably the best we can do from a long-term perspective. Many potential challenges in the future can be mitigated by our decision now. If we don't react in the business direction and communicate pros and cons, we can quickly get into a situation of building never-ending MVP or never-ending experimentation (described in 3.4.1 Regular re-evaluation of the three axes as a continuous process). We also need to prepare stakeholders because the industrialization of an ad-hoc solution could take a significant time or require complex redesign. In some cases, it could even be impossible due to technical (e.g., IT tools availability) or even conceptual (e.g., data security) challenges.

4.1.1   Moving on the analytics journey for ad-hoc AA projects

Table 4.2 shows the evolution of the ad-hoc advanced analytics project compared to different types of analytics (from predictive to cognitive). We just highlighted the metrics that changed; all others are empty.

		Risk rate		Com-ments
		Predictive	Cognitive	
Three-Axis Approach				
Analytics Maturity	Stakeholder Maturity	Low	High	**A**
	Company Analytics Maturity	Low	High	**A**
	Analytics Landscape Maturity	Low	High	**A**
	Market	Low	Medium	**A**
Data Maturity	Are data available	Low	Medium	
	Are data integrated			
	Are data described			
	Is data security clear			
IT Maturity	Are tools available			
	Are tools integrated			
	Are tools flexible			
	Are processes established			
	Access to Toolset			
	Best Practices			
	Deployment Standards			
	Support Models			
	Delivery Model			
Common Attributes				
Agile x Waterfall				
Data-driven				
Technology Mix				
Data Oriented Thinking				
Maintenance of Analytics				
Prototyping and Experimentation				
Challenges				
Management Expectations		Medium	High	**B**
WoW		Low	Low	
Industrialization Challenge		Low (Medium)	Low (High)	**B**
Time Impact				
Time Impact				

*Table 4.2: Risk evaluation for moving on the advanced
analytics journey – from predictive to cognitive*

A As we move on the analytics maturity axis, the common understanding of the analytical approach decreases. The algorithms are becoming more complex and less easy to explain in "plain" language to non-data science people. That leads to a higher level of resistance to accepting the results. Basically, this statement is valid across stakeholder maturity, company maturity, and even the general market. To reiterate, we need to have acceptance on every single level to manage the project successfully. For example, we can have good stakeholder maturity (the stakeholder could even have a data science background), but they will not be able to persuade others in the company to invest in the analytics solution – they will not get the budget approved. The market could be a significant influencer as well – if other companies are investing and sharing positive results, there will be a higher probability of willingness to invest in an analytics project as well.

B As we move in analytics maturity from predictive to cognitive, the risk around "management expectation" and the "industrialization challenge" could increase. That is caused mainly by the fact that fewer projects were implemented in more advanced analytical areas (on the right side of the analytics maturity axis), meaning less experience exists with the management of such a project. Compared with risk A, this risk is not about the result acceptance due to lower analytical method transparency, but it is connected with less experience with the project itself. It is human nature to extrapolate experiences of earlier projects and try to use and leverage them for current work. This approach sometimes means that we see predictive projects as the same as cognitive projects – which is not necessarily true (you can see that we partly also use this extrapolation in this book when talking about advanced analytics projects in general). There could be significant differences between the available tools (both in the company and within the market) and the WoW (for example, the ratio between experimentation and industrialization could differ). Also, there are fewer experienced people on the market to deliver such a project. If you combine the statement above with the hype currently resonating around artificial intelligence and machine learning approaches, you can get a "danger" combination that could be challenging for the project from many perspectives.

4.2 Robust descriptive analytics projects (data are ready)

Table 4.3 shows the evaluation of the risks, challenges, and commonalities for Robust descriptive analytics when data are ready.

		Risk rate	Comments
Three-Axis Approach			
Analytics Maturity	Stakeholder Maturity	Low	
	Company Analytics Maturity	Low	
	Analytics Landscape Maturity	Low	
	Market	Low	
Data Maturity	Are data available	Medium	
	Are data integrated	Medium	
	Are data described	Medium	**A**
	Is data security clear	Medium	**B**

	Are tools available	Low	
	Are tools integrated	Low	
	Are tools flexible	Medium	**C**
	Are processes established		
IT Maturity	Access to Toolset	Low	
	Best Practices	Low	
	Deployment Standards	Low	
	Support Models	Medium	
	Delivery Model	Medium	**D**
Common Attributes			
Agile x Waterfall		Low	**E**
Data-driven		Low	**E**
Technology Mix		Low	**E**
Data Oriented Thinking		Low	**E**
Maintenance of Analytics		Low	**E**
Prototyping and Experimentation		Low	**E**
Challenges			
Management Expectations		Low	**E**
WoW		Low	**E**
Industrializa-tion Challenge		Low	**E**
Time Impact			
Time Impact		Low	**E**

Table 4.3: Risk evaluation for typical robust descriptive analytics project (data are ready)

The assumption could be wrong:

In general, the biggest problem in this project type could be the project type definition – a wrong assumption. The claim that data storage is ready is strong, but we may find that it is not entirely true. It does not need to be on a scale where data are unavailable, but data could be available in the wrong formats/structures. That means either we need to include data modellers/engineers into the project (and we need to synchronize with the data storage lifecycle) or do the transformation in the reporting tool. As you can imagine, both limit the project delivery.

There could also be an impact from the time perspective. Data could be available at the beginning of the project, but we may find that additional data need to be involved as we move forward. That could mean a significant change in the delivery mode, especially in the delivery speed. As stakeholders are used to some release pace (of reports), slowing down (due to data tasks that need to be fulfilled) could lead to considerable pressure on making a shortcut in the IT landscape (for example, loading data directly into the reporting tool and making the data transformation there). Integrating additional data sources could generate a substantial increase in the funding necessary to deliver business results, which would not have been available otherwise.

A As we highlighted above in the data maturity section, the fact that data are available and accessible for use does not necessarily mean that we can easily leverage them right away. A lack of data understanding is a typical obstacle, which deserves attention.

We should look for information not just on whether the desired data are ingested in the data storage but also for documentation about the data (metadata). If there is none, it increases the risk of unknown issues with leveraging the data. These are a few more signs:

— data have not yet been integrated
— no consumer has used the data yet
— data set column names are not self-explanatory
— there is no data steward or subject matter person assigned to the data

When performing such an evaluation, we should be granular enough in the analysis to avoid misunderstandings. For example, we can do a project which requires actual sales data and learn that sales data are available in the data storage/feed ABC, which a different project has successfully leveraged. Later we learn that the previous project leveraged gross sales, but we need net sales, and the feed ABC does not contain net sales.

In an ideal world (high data maturity), all data would be perfectly described (business, technical, operational metadata, data lineage…), but this is rarely the case. Therefore, we should set up a strong collaboration with the data steward or another subject expert who has deep working experience with the data we will be leveraging in the reporting project.

The situation might become more complex if the reporting project goes across multiple divisions or regions because definitions can vary across business entities and can be challenging to synchronize. E.g., when you ask for net sales in one country or division, you can get different numbers than in another because the business might operate differently and, e.g., the business logic for deductions is different. You can have timely stakeholder discussions about standardization or localization if you know of such variations, as they can significantly influence the scope and solution approach.

B Data security, in this case, should be an observed item because it can be appropriately set up on the data storage level (and hence not considered a required activity), but the reporting component can introduce new requirements. For example, in some reports, we will combine data from various Datamart tables with different security, or new user groups will be created that are only allowed to see selected attributes. We should spot such business requirements as it not only affects the reporting scope but, in some cases, it might impact data storage as well, depending on the data and solution architecture.

C If we are developing reports in the out-of-the-box modern BI tool, the features will be limited by this tool, but we will be rewarded by the speed of delivery, scalability, and maintainability of such a solution. That is not surprising but let us provide two recommendations when going for an out-of-the-box solution:

— Try to identify top business requirements that could be game-changers and impact the tool selection, as you ideally do not want to switch the tool during project development. An example of how it could go wrong: IT and business agree on the reporting tool, the project team develops the solution and then finds out that a critical functionality is embedding analytical insights into other pages. The selected tool does not have such a functionality, or it is constrained.

— Educate stakeholders – provide training in the tool; show them the limitations as well as the art of the feasible.

In any situation, it is good to understand the tool's flexibility (as the project is developing over time, so any analysis made at the beginning could change). We need to communicate with business users about what adding a specific visualization into the solution could mean. It could be on the following scale:

1. Not possible at all. Any specific visualization could mean a change in the reporting tool.
2. It is potentially possible but expensive and not proven. Some experimentation needs to be done.
3. It is possible – it is not recommended as it is not standard, but there are proven ways to do it.

Based on the position on this scale, we need to choose a suitable communication model with stakeholders.

D There is often a centralized reporting team responsible for the delivery and maintenance of reporting solutions. One may say what potential risk there can be. Business requests report(s), IT delivers them and operates them. However, it does not usually work like that, even when the solution is not rocket science. With some exceptions, there needs to be an interaction between the delivery team and business as more requirements can simply come later and change the original solution. Many reporting projects failed in the past due to the wrong delivery model (way of working). These failures were caused by iteration with business, a lack of business feedback or time impact, even though business saw the solution for the first time after a long development period. For such reasons, business seeks more efficient processes for providing the requested solutions in the right time and quality. As a result, we see the trend of moving development from the centralized reporting team to business itself. IT is needed just for deployment to the production environment, maintenance, or support for technical challenges. If such a development respects company standards and best practices, there is probably no issue. As you can imagine, this may cause a different (the opposite) type of challenge. It is possible that business developers do not follow IT standards at all for several reasons (for example, the speed of development or a lack of knowledge). The developed solution may not even be possible to deploy to the production (as it does not necessarily meet all the attributes for stability, long term maintenance or performance), or there is a significant need for industrialization. That could considerably influence the time when the solution becomes available for users.

E As you can see in the overall picture, we do not consider any common attributes or challenges a critical risk for this type of project. The prototyping aspect could be slightly challenging, but it should be easy to explain. Also, as this is quite a common and well-known project type, there is already a great deal of experience. Due to that, expectation management is also easier to achieve. The size of the project (the area or domain in which we are implementing a new reporting solution) could be a significant factor of complexity. There could be many challenges in agreeing on a joint approach across regions or products, for example. Therefore, business alignment is critical and could significantly influence the timelines of overall delivery. However, this is a well-known and expected complexity, so we do not consider it a critical risk. Business involvement and alignment are key for every analytics project.

If data preparation is out of the scope of such a project, it could mean that another project needs to prepare the data for consumption. That could be a critical dependency, and we may only have a minimal possibility to influence and manage the relationship. If we find ourselves in this situation, we need to closely monitor the dependency as any change could significantly impact delivery.

4.3 Robust descriptive analytics project (data are not ready)

Table 4.4 shows the evaluation of the risks, challenges, and commonalities for Robust descriptive analytics when data are not ready.

		Risk rate	Comments
Three-Axis Approach			
Analytics Maturity	Stakeholder Maturity	Medium	**A**
	Company Analytics Maturity	Low	
	Analytics Landscape Maturity	Low	
	Market	Low	
Data Maturity	Are data available	Medium	**B**
	Are data integrated	Medium	**B**
	Are data described	High	**B**
	Is data security clear	Medium	**B**
IT Maturity	Are tools available	Low	**D**
	Are tools integrated	Medium	**C**
	Are tools flexible	Low	
	Are processes established		
	Access to Toolset	Low	**D**
	Best Practices	Low	
	Deployment Standards	Low	**C**
	Support Models	Low	
	Delivery Model	Low	**C**
Common Attributes			
Agile x Waterfall		Medium	**F**
Data-driven		Medium	**E**
Technology Mix		Medium	**C**
Data Oriented Thinking		Medium	**E**
Maintenance of Analytics		Low	
Prototyping and Experimentation		Medium	**F**
Challenges			
Management Expectations		Medium	**E**
WoW		Medium	**G**
Industrialization Challenge		Low	**F**
Time Impact			
Time Impact		Low	

Table 4.4: Risk evaluation for typical robust descriptive analytics project (data are not ready)

A Unlike the previous project type, this one includes the data preparation portion. As data management activities play a significant role and can take up to 80 % of effort on such a typical project, there are two watch items related to stakeholder maturity here.

First, part of stakeholder maturity is seeing the value of having data available for analytics in the robust approach. That is relevant not only during project initiation; alignment on value between stakeholders and the technical team is critical throughout the project (e.g., during the prioritization of work). However, this gets easily neglected because the outcomes of data preparation work are more challenging to present than fancy dashboards.

Second, stakeholders' understanding of the delivery complexity of data engineering work also reduces the risk of "bad surprises". We described more of these challenges in the chapter 3.1 Key challenges in managing stakeholders' expectations.

Suppose this stakeholder maturity is low and not adequately compensated by solid communication with the delivery team. In that case, it can lead to many failures – e.g., deprioritized data engineering activities resulting in too much technical debt, which is hard to absorb, unrealistic expectations on the delivery time, etc.

B As this project type is heavily data-driven and the data are the key, most data maturity axis considerations could apply here. Particular attention should be paid to all dependencies on data sources subject to acquisition on this project. Are the data available? Can we connect to the data sources (technically, legally...)? Do we understand the data, or do we have resources to help with understanding the data? If the data provider is not ready to provide data, the project may not even start.

When data preparation is in the scope of reporting, we should also clarify whether data storage is a key result (value) of the project. Data storage (regardless of the technical solution) enables reporting, and hence it has value in any case, but the question here is whether it has a key value on its own. Are we building a solution solely for the currently known reporting requirements, or are we building an analytics repository that can be consumed even by other projects/data consumers in the future? Is it expected to integrate and harmonize the data in the analytics repository? The answers to these questions will affect the priority of various activities as well as the solution designs.

C We are also pinpointing potential risks in this project type's technology mix and deployment standards. As we cover the process almost end to end here, starting by accessing and managing data and ending with their presentation, we will logically use different tools. As these project's parts look "independent" – the reporting tool does not care much about data transformation – we can encounter various issues connected with the architecture, best practices, and standards. For example, we can only read specific parts of the database dedicated to reporting, and we need to use a dedicated account. Objects in the database must have certain characteristics like a naming convention or access provisioning. If we cannot use any object from "our" database, we will be limited and slowed down during the whole development. On the other hand, if we can read any object for the purposes of our prototype, how difficult is it to meet deployment standards? And when is the right time to consider them?

Another example of technology complexity could be security implementation across different tools or a single sign-on set-up. But it can go even further. More technologies mean that we need to have more experts on the team, more support teams could be required, or we need more ways to solve technical problems (on the other hand, we have a great deal of flexibility). This combination leads to a more complex team and delivery management. Experimentation and prototyping aspects may also change the WoW in the same technology. This complexity could be challenging to understand even for technical developers focused on one tool, so investment in alignment across the experts with different approaches needs to be high. That means a great deal of time (money) might be invested in non-development work just because of the technical setup.

D For companies with well-positioned analytics and IT maturity, this type of project will probably not cause any challenges initially (assuming point B caused nothing serious). This is just another project from many that the company has successfully completed in the past with processes and technological stack optimization based on lessons learned meetups. If there is no reason not to do so, the next project will use the same processes and common architecture. A different case is when some part has not been implemented (tried) yet. The establishment of new processes and technologies is always a challenge, and one must consider many aspects and comply with company strategy, vision, and other projects running in parallel working on similar goals. The right decision and direction are not easy. Selecting specific (right) technology is a complex discipline that will significantly impact analytical direction in future, beyond the project itself, like high costs for licenses and hardware, establishment of new processes or development principles. Equally, risks exist for changing key infrastructure or processes in the project itself.

E Preparation of data is a complex task that is usually hidden behind fancy visualisation. But visualisation will provide business value only when displayed data are correct. Presenting reports with inaccurate data is the easiest way to lose the trust of users. That is why we need to focus on data understanding and connect this with business knowledge. The problem is that you cannot prepare the solution only for the combination of data that is valid today. For example, you need to join two product code tables from two different systems. Today, it could look like an easy ask – we can have a 100% fit, so each product is mapped accordingly, and there are no problems. But will this situation stay that way in the following months? Could there be a situation in future when there will be a product in one system that is not in the second one? Or vice versa? And even worse, is it possible that there will be different product names in each system or different levels of hierarchies in the future? If yes, how should the system behave (from a business perspective)? Anytime a data engineer develops a data pipeline, they need to realize what other situation could occur in the future and design the pipeline accordingly. If it is not appropriately designed, the dashboard could display incorrect data in the future – even though the solution would technically be running without any problem (data pipelines are running with technical errors). As you can imagine, this is a complex and time-consuming task.

And it also requires people who are not only technical experts but those who can talk with business people to discuss the combination that could occur and understand what needs to happen from a business perspective if such a situation arises. As you are working with potential problems (which may not be visible in the data today), you need to have a very experienced team (the easiest way to define potential issues is based on the experiences from other projects) with abstract thinking capabilities. So, you need to look for people who have technology expertise, have an abstract thinking approach, and can talk with business to explain the abstract problem and transform it into the business language.

If we underestimate the problem, we are creating "hidden" technical debt in the solution – maybe it could be better to say "data" debt in this situation. That is why we have also connected this with "management expectation" – as you need to explain it to stakeholders and find a consensus about the "data" quality and delivery speed of the solution. And as usual, none of the extremes are good.

F The prototyping approach is of great help in the delivery. Unfortunately, it relates to the industrialization challenge. We can even say that the more prototyping is done, the more challenging the industrialization process. From a prototyping perspective, the following factors are in play:

Number of prototypes

Not every prototype will move to the industrialization phase. But the ones that will be industrialized usually need to be redesigned. As such, more prototypes could mean more rework. In this case, the economies of scale do not apply as much – every single prototype could be designed differently and need to be explained. Ideally, the prototyping and industrialization teams should be the same; otherwise, a communication challenge will also be inevitable.

The technical solution for prototyping

The technical landscape for prototyping is also critical. The prototyping could be done in highly different tools, so redesign might not even be possible sometimes. Commonly, prototyping starts with drawing on the flipchart. A high-level visual appearance of the report is captured and discussed in detail later. Imagine that this will be done by someone who does not know the technology used for industrialization – it could easily lead to a situation where some visual concepts will not be possible to implement in the tool. The end-user experience should be the most critical aspect (after all, what use is a report that nobody is using). On the other hand, we need to understand that there could be quite a high price that must be paid (we have discussed it from an IT perspective in the chapter 1.3.3 Are the tools flexible?).

Moreover, this project is data-driven – so we need to combine the UI perspective with the data perspective.

The opposite could be the case: that we are using the same tool for prototyping as for industrialization or we have a migration process set up. That could help us a lot as then the industrialization process could be much easier. However, even in this situation, you need to understand and evaluate whether the approach (technical) used for prototyping (the main goal is the speed of delivery) is viable also for the robust use case (when the main goal is performance and stability). However, if you have the same tool, the technical implementation could still be significantly different. So, although you can migrate from a prototype environment to a robust one, you will not do it as a technical redesign is needed.

Data solution for prototyping

Data preparation complexity is another aspect of prototyping. We have described data complexity in the previous point, so let us just summarize the difference. In prototyping, the goal is speed – you do not need to solve all potential data issues if they do not affect the visual (for example, the number of products could dramatically influence the report's design). During the industrialization process, you need to analyse all the data combinations (even if they are not in the data at the given moment) to ensure solution stability from the data perspective.

As we are usually forced to speed up the delivery during the project, it is wise to expect that we will be pushed to use the prototype more. That could happen even for work that the prototype should not be used for, like deploying prototypes into the production environment. Using the right approach for the right phase of the project is critical for the project success and for the future development of the project (this could be very limited by technical/data debt generated in the first phases of the project).

G   The WoW is complex as multiple teams are involved. Cooperation within the data engineering and data visualisation teams could be especially complicated to manage, as they have different paces and concepts of work.

The most complex project to manage is a combination of the "robust descriptive analytics project" with AA work. In the chapter 3.2.4 WoW – Analytics ecosystem (including AA), we have briefly discussed what it means to include AA work into the scope. It is difficult to highlight the main potential risk for such a combination in such a case, as this is really the combination of all previous ones. The challenges and approaches are so different that it is impossible to manage them in the same way and compare one with another. And this is precisely the biggest potential risk that we see there.

We need to realize and explain that different project parts are managed differently, focusing on different aspects in different streams. We need to explain this not only to stakeholders (which is critical) but also to the delivery team as there could be internal competition. We need to define different WoWs, standards, technical maturity – simply everything we discussed in the book. The team needs to understand that just because another team works differently, their work is not necessarily better or worse. On the other hand, we should make sure the difference in work is not used as an excuse by the delivery team. We need to set up an environment of cooperation and respect in which teams learn one from another and try to move and improve the delivery model together.

4.4   Industrialization risks

In the whole book, we have been focusing on the differences between ad-hoc and robust projects and potentially on the challenges connected with the move from ad-hoc solutions to robust ones. We want to summarize this "industrialization challenge" from the risk perspective as well. It is important to remember that we are not evaluating the project as such – we are focusing on the move from ad-hoc to robust – which is an entirely different perspective. You can have an excellent and easy ad-hoc project, but it may simply not be ready for industrialization. From a different angle – if you are doing a robust project, there should not be any industrialization challenge risks (which may still happen due to the prototyping and experimentations concepts).

For this summary specifically, we will compare the differences within the analytics maturity axis. You may see a different risk evaluation for the descriptive vs advanced analytics projects, which could help you manage the risk better. All the information should be available in other parts of the book, so let us look at this part as consolidated information (Table 4.5).

| | | Risk rate | | Com-ments |
		Descrip-tive	Advanced Analytics	
Three-Axis Approach				
Analytics Maturity	Stakeholder Maturity	Medium	High	**A**
	Company Analytics Maturity	Medium	High	**A**
	Analytics Landscape Maturity	Medium	High	**A**
	Market	Low	High	**A**
Data Maturity	Are data available	Low	Low	
	Are data integrated	High	High	**B**
	Are data described	Medium	High	**B**
	Is data security clear	Medium	High	**B**
IT Maturity	Are tools available	Low	High	**C**
	Are tools integrated	Low	High	**C**
	Are tools flexible	Low	Medium	**C**

IT Maturity	Are processes established			
	Access to Toolset	Low	High	**D**
	Best Practices	Medium	High	**D**
	Deployment Standards	Medium	High	**D**
	Support Models	Medium	High	**D**
	Delivery Model	Medium	High	**D**
Common Attributes				
Agile x Waterfall		Low	Low	**G**
Data-driven		High	High	**E**
Technology Mix		Medium	Medium	**F**
Data Oriented Thinking		High	High	**E**
Maintenance of Analytics		Low	High	**H**
Prototyping and Experimentation		Medium	Medium	**G**
Challenges				
Management Expectations		Medium	Medium	**I**
WoW		Low	Low	
Industrialization Challenge		NA	NA	
Time Impact				
Time Impact		NA	NA	**J**

Table 4.5: Risk evaluation for industrialization for typical descriptive vs advanced analytics projects

A The main challenge in this area could be understanding the industrialization processes. Not everyone has the experience of what industrialization may mean and how complex it can be. As we mentioned, it could mean a complex redesign that needs to follow IT processes and standards. That could be challenging from both the financial perspective (for example, a significant part of the solution must be refactored, additional licenses could be needed) and the time perspective (which could materialize either as needing more time or more money). Moreover, a different WoW may need to be used. Altogether, it could be challenging to accept in the project as the ad-hoc approach has a considerably different speed and concept of delivery. So, compared to a robust approach, it could be considered a step back from agile to waterfall. It only reflects the actual complexity of analytics project delivery and the cost of "technical debt removal", as we mentioned for ad-hoc.

Specifically for the projects on the right side of analytics maturity, there are more risks. Less experience and a lower number of projects in this area mean additional challenges – specifically the assumption that all advanced analytics projects are the same. That could set up many wrong expectations even if we consider industrialization as part of the project from the beginning. It could be better to deal with industrialization as a "first of a kind" project than apply assumptions irrelevant in the respective area.

B Data integration specifically is challenging. For ad-hoc projects, you do not need to address all potential challenges with the data integration. It is enough to integrate data for one specific purpose (and only one time), not thinking about all the combinations (data combinations) that could arise. Moreover, it can be done manually, so the business logic implemented does not need to be comprehensive. During industrialization, we need to automatize everything, so the business logic needs to be described in detail – or manual steps need to be included.

Data description could be challenging because we need to generate additional metadata during industrialization. Metadata should include information on the transformation (technical, operational, and business) and the result/artefact generated (report description or analytical model description). This forces business owners to be precise and agree on every calculation and metrics definition.

Specifically for advanced analytics projects, we need to describe not only the artefacts generated (the advanced analytics model itself) but also the new data derived. It may be as complex as a business and technical description of any other source system providing data into the ecosystem. The granularity level for metadata description depends on IT standards and could be a requirement of the production deployment.

C For the tool evaluation, you can see a difference for each extreme of the analytics axis. For descriptive, tools are usually available and well established. That does not mean we do not need to redesign since the toolset (its deployment standards) could be different for the ad-hoc and robust approaches, but the toolset is usually ready.

In the advanced analytics space, the problem could be more complex. As there are fewer projects, tools are probably not well established in the IT ecosystem. Therefore, industrialisation could include establishing a standard advanced analytics tool in the company, which moves us from the analytics project more to the side of the IT project.

D An "established process" can help in general, but it can also bring complexity. During the ad-hoc development, not only is it necessary to use the right tool – it could be equally important to use it in the right way. Otherwise, we can find that we are not authorized to deploy into production or have no support. Again, it is more likely the problem will occur in advanced analytics project industrialization, as tools are not so well established and best practices are not commonly known very well (and could be largely company dependent).

E Data must be managed differently in many cases for the robust (industrialized) projects than for ad-hoc, so the project will invest some effort to achieve standards. What does this mean? While in the ad-hoc project, we can simply use "any" data in "any" structures, we need to think through every attribute of data maturity during industrialisation. Data description and data integration might be optional in terms of analytics maturity and the type of industrialization project, but for instance, the question of data availability and security plays a more significant role here, whether we like it or not. Data we need can be difficult to access in a standard manner or may introduce the need for standardized objects, connectors, or ingestion methods. In security, our outcomes will be consumed by various audiences with varied visibility based on organization unit and role. Advanced analytics models often deliver (generate) new data that must be considered in the security setup as well. If industrialization represents complex data integration (and data description), we need to onboard more dedicated resources or cooperate with other projects if data integration is part of their delivery.

F In the case of technology mix – which we also include as one risk during industrialization – the situation is simple. Regular tools (platforms) are not used correctly, or the target platform for industrialization does not offer a good level of support for all our requirements. The project must ideally use what the company's IT landscape allows, is widely used, and is supported in a regular way. If we introduce a new tool or platform, we are bringing further complexity for industrialization consisting of deploying new technology and the processes around it. In many cases, company architects or financial factors will stop the deployment of a new tool. Then we may have no other choice than to continue with industrialization in the available tools and address all the challenges that can occur. We cannot face any issues and challenges for our industrialization right away (while moving the ad-hoc project to robust). However, as we had planned the industrialization on a specific platform, we may encounter new challenges later, so we recommend summarizing some principles for future change management and avoiding refactoring, significant changes, or migration to another technology caused by platform limitations.

G In general, industrialization introduces more substantial dependencies into the delivery system, influencing the balance within the agile x waterfall concepts. Mainly, this relates to:

— Data – data need to be ingested and comprehensively analysed first
— You need to potentially redesign prototypes or even realize and explain that what was delivered were "only" prototypes.

Dependencies mean new WoWs and a different point of view on crucial decisions. You may need to re-evaluate the balance between the speed of prototyping and industrialization time. These aspects could significantly influence the pace of the project and the overall team set-up. They may not only change the team structure but also significantly influence the balance of skillsets in the team. For instance, more "data" oriented people may be needed (data engineers for data preparation tasks).

H For industrialized descriptive analytical projects, we should be covered in terms of maintenance. We have data ingestion, reports updating regularly (basically using some task flow once data ingestion is done), and periodically shared or consumed by users. Except for some exceptions and more extensive customizations (deviations from known standards), we are not expecting any issues, as we are following years of proven practices. For advanced analytics projects, the situation will be quite different, and maintenance can cause new challenges and complexity, and more so for solutions that have not been introduced in the company yet. The development team will likely have to define new standards and processes to maintain AA models and prepare support scenarios for operations. In many cases, we need to distinguish configuration changes (for model calibration that can be done quickly without deployment) and changes that require deployment to a higher environment (change in code) and setup. By the end of the day, we need to provide extra knowledge transfer to the operational team. The project needs to communicate maintenance requirements in advance so the operations team has adequate and sufficient resources to support us.

I Management of expectation is connected mainly with the speed of delivery and team size. Industrialization usually means that the project will slow down, and we may need to invest more money into robust concepts (especially if we are not following recommended best practices from the beginning). In the beginning, it could also mean redesigning the existing solution – which does not bring immediate business benefits. We need to be able to explain that industrialization has benefits other than additional/new insight. If we have established open communication with stakeholders from the beginning, this should not be a problem.

The real challenge could be that industrialization means restricting the functionality – we cannot fully industrialise the prototype. Multiple factors may cause this. For example, the scale of industrialization (number of users/data) could mean that tools are not performing enough, requiring significant redesign or limitations. Or we can find that the toolset that we have for a robust solution does not include the analytics method we would like to use. Constant monitoring of the project development can help us avoid such a situation.

J We consider industrialization a result of time impact. As the project evolves over time (or maybe the understanding of the project), the road may lead to industrialization. We just would like to highlight that this is a natural and healthy process – we just need to be able to manage it properly.

5 Typical questions for analytics projects

As the last chapter of the book, we will try to provide you with some examples of questions that could be asked of relevant people in order to analyse the project . These questions may help you properly position the project on to each axis and understand the commonalities and general project challenges. This serves only as an example and may differ a great deal based on your company and environment.

Analytics Maturity

ANALYTICS MATURITY IN GENERAL:

- [ ] *To what analytics solution, product, or service does your analytics project contribute?*
- [ ] *Which other elements of the analytics landscape play an important role in the case of your project? Which stakeholders, market conditions, etc.?*
- [ ] *Do you have reports at your disposal?*
- [ ] *Do you have data at your disposal regularly?*
- [ ] *Are any additional insights generated automatically? How?*
- [ ] *Have you established a planning process?*
- [ ] *Which metrics are regularly planned?*
- [ ] *Is there any automation in the planning process?*
- [ ] *How do you address potential future problems? Is it mainly an expert decision? Which support techniques does management have?*
- [ ] *Are the support techniques embedded into the regular reporting process?*
- [ ] *Do reports contain any recommendations for future steps?*
- [ ] *Are you able to describe how recommendations are generated/provided?*
- [ ] *Do you trust the recommendations? Are the recommendations*

a mandatory part of the planning process?

☐ **STAKEHOLDER ANALYTICS MATURITY:**
☐ *How do you gain insight into the business situation?*
☐ *Do you have a standard way of analysing your business?*
☐ *How much time do you need to update your insight? Is the insight even updated automatically? Are you willing to invest in automation? Does it even make sense?*
☐ *Have you ever asked for a prediction of any metrics?*
☐ *Have you ever implemented prediction results into the business process?*
☐ *Do you use any predictions repeatedly?*
☐ *Do you believe in advanced analytics methods? Are you ready to automatize some decisions entirely based on the algorithm recommendation?*
☐ *Do you think that human expertise is always needed to make a decision?*
☐ *Do you think that a human always needs to double-check automated decisions?*

☐ **COMPANY ANALYTICS MATURITY:**
☐ *In your perspective, is the company data-driven?*
☐ *Would you categorize your company as innovative?*
☐ *Is the analytics solution category a regular part of the budget?*
☐ *If you provide enough data, can you achieve budget increase?*
☐ *Are you willing to shift parts of your budget into different departments based on the analytics results (because you can be sure that the reverse will also happen in the future)?*
☐ *How would you compare your company with the market from an analytical perspective?*
☐ *Did any disruption occur in the recent past concerning analytics in the industry?*
☐ *Do you have a dedicated data/reporting team?*

☐ **ANALYTICS LANDSCAPE MATURITY:**
☐ *Can you describe KPIs (metrics) that you monitor regularly?*
☐ *Are the KPIs (metrics) generated automatically?*
☐ *Is a description of the KPIs (metrics) available?*
☐ *Do you have any automatized prediction models?*
☐ *Do you have data available for any type of analysis you would like to run?*
☐ *Do you have integrated data?*
☐ *Can you show us a list of products/regions/... with descriptions? Does everyone in your department use this list? Is this list used companywide?*
☐ *Does your company have a data warehouse or any analytical database?*

Data Maturity

■ **ARE DATA AVAILABLE?**
☐ *Do you know where data are stored physically?*
☐ *Do you know how to access them?*
☐ *Do you know the granularity of the data?*
☐ *Has someone already used the required data set for analysis?*
☐ *Do you know the team that is managing the source system?*
☐ *Do you know the data formats?*
☐ *Do you know how often the data are updated?*
☐ *Is data provided using any service, e.g., Data as a Service or API?*
☐ *Is there any agreement or contract with the data source provided on the data provisioning?*

■ **ARE DATA INTEGRATED?**
☐ *Has anyone used the data before with some other data set?*
☐ *Do you know the definition of dimensions across the data sources?*
☐ *Are you sure that the data format in the two source systems is the same?*
☐ *Are you sure that the granularity of data in the two source systems is the same?*
☐ *Do you know how the source systems tackle the time dimension?*
☐ *Is any DWH solution in place?*
☐ *What is the company strategy for integrated data?*
☐ *What is the delivery model for DWH? Is there a central team in place?*
☐ *Is the integrated data a valuable result of analytics projects in general?*

■ **ARE DATA DESCRIBED?**
☐ *Is there a central solution for describing analytics artefacts (report, KPI, tables…) within the company?*
☐ *Do you know the standard definition of metrics used in the department/company?*
☐ *Does the source system include a described interface for data consumption?*
☐ *Has the source system ever provided data sets to someone else?*
☐ *Do you have a contact for the "data owner"?*
☐ *Does the "data owner" or "data steward" role even exist in the company?*
☐ *Is there a guideline that describes the approach to metadata? Is it for technical, operational, or business metadata?*
☐ *Does the export of the data include any log files?*
☐ *Do you know how often data are updated?*
☐ *How quick or straightforward is it to get or find an answer regarding the business meaning of the data?*
☐ *Are there data models in place? (conceptual, logical, physical)*

☐ *Do you have access to the documentation of business and technological transformations in existing data pipelines relevant to your project?*

■ **IS DATA SECURITY CONSIDERED?**
☐ *Is there a security model that is described in general?*
☐ *Is there a security model that is described for concrete data sets?*
☐ *Can I use the data set? What are the restrictions?*
☐ *Can I share the data set? What are the restrictions?*
☐ *At which level of granularity would you like to share the data?*
☐ *Will any sensitive data (personal ID, credit card....) be available for the end-users?*
☐ *Will there be any sensitive data in the data sources?*
☐ *Has anyone used the same data before? Was this data shared across the company?*
☐ *Do the data move across regions?*
☐ *Does the company have GDPR guidance?*
☐ *Has there been a similar project that implemented similar security restrictions during the implementation?*
☐ *Is the security requirement a standard part of IT guidelines?*
☐ *Does my data/report storage comply with security standards?*
☐ *What do I need to comply with security standards?*

IT Maturity

■ **ARE THE TOOLS AVAILABLE?**
☐ *What tool do we have for... (data preparation, data modelling...)?*
☐ *What is the license model for the tool?*
☐ *Is there any limitation on how to use the existing toolset?*
☐ *What toolset was used by the last similar analytics project and why?*
☐ *Do the standard tools cover every analytical step?*
☐ *Are the tools scalable enough in the case that the project will bring a significant additional performance demand?*
☐ *Is the tool stable enough (LTS vs Beta, education edition vs enterprise)?*
☐ *Is a tool knowledge base available?*
☐ *Is any particular experience needed to start using the tool?*
☐ *Is it an in-premise or in-cloud solution?*
☐ *Is the tool provided as PaaS or SaaS?*

ARE THE TOOLS INTEGRATED?
- Were the recommended tools used together on some analytics projects?
- Are the boundaries between the tools defined? Are there best practices on when to use which tool?
- Is there a single security model for all the tools that should be used?
- Is it possible to access tools outside of the company network?
- What methods are used for integration? (e.g., API, microservice concept)

ARE THE TOOLS FLEXIBLE?
- Does the tool have varied interfaces (data connectors, support for API)?
- Is the tool just WYSIWYG, or does it enable developers to use coding and customize using scripts and parameters?
- Is the tool based on architecture supporting development swarming?
- Is it possible to add custom components to the tools?
- Is there a list of custom components already added to the ecosystem?
- Is there a central team taking care of the custom component?
- Is there a described process (methodology, standards) of how to do it?
- How difficult is it to add a custom component?

ARE PROCESSES ESTABLISHED?
- Is the tool supported? Does the support also extend to added custom components?
- What kind of support is commonly available – infrastructure, data, analytics model?
- Is monitoring established?
- Is there a single support contact for the projects?
- Is there any limitation in the tool usage? Are components missing in the tool in comparison with the market offer?
- How quickly can you get access to the tool? What is the approval process?
- What are the development processes that need to be followed?
- What are the deployment processes that need to be followed?
- Is there a central team that oversees the deployment?
- What is the required documentation? Is an example of the documentation available?
- How much involvement of a central team in the development is needed? Is there a competence centre that could help?
- What is the tool lifecycle, and what is the update roadmap?
- Does the tool support version control, and is version control in place?

■ **AD-HOC X ROBUST**
- [ ] *Is it an ad-hoc problem?*
- [ ] *Is it an ad-hoc need?*
- [ ] *How likely is it that the same problem/question will need to be addressed next month?*
- [ ] *In case you can have the same analytics support available regularly, would it make sense for you?*
- [ ] *Is the analytics problem significant enough to invest money into automation?*
- [ ] *Do you expect that running the analysis next time will be easier and quicker? Why do you think so?*

Other

Below you can find fundamental questions for evaluating how ready the team is to follow the recommendations included in this book. It is quite high-level as this is not the focus of this book, but it could still be valuable as a starting point for a conversation with the team. It is mainly connected with WoW.

■ **TEAM READINESS**
- [ ] *Does the experience profile of the team match with the analytics project type?*
- [ ] *Do the non-technical professionals (scrum masters, project managers...) have experience with analytics projects?*
- [ ] *Are team members focused on one area, or do they have experiences from several types of analytical tasks?*
- [ ] *Are the data engineers and data scientists willing to stretch themselves beyond their current focus and experience?*
- [ ] *Does the team understand the value of data reusability?*
- [ ] *Does the team understand the complexity of industrialization?*
- [ ] *Is there a strong preference for one technology? If yes, is the reason for such a preference well justified?*
- [ ] *Does the team understand the business goal of the project?*
- [ ] *Are the team members even interested in the business goals?*
- [ ] *Is there an understanding of the relationship between technical tasks and business goals?*
- [ ] *Are the members ready to talk with business (users, sponsors...)?*
- [ ] *How are the business users represented in the project team?*
- [ ] *Do the business users wish to help with development?*
- [ ] *How are tasks prioritized?*
- [ ] *How often are meetings between business and the technical team organized?*
- [ ] *Do you have an expert on data in the team?*
- [ ] *How engaged are the data owners in the project?*

Conclusion

Congratulations!

You are at the end of this book, and we believe that – even if some of the information contained in this book was not wholly new – you are at least taking away some new advice and ideas that can help you manage your analytics for success.

In the first part of the book, we described analytics project categorization from the three-axis point of view, including a look at analytics maturity, data maturity and IT maturity, illustrating the maturity levels of the three pillars of analytics. We also highlighted the differences between ad-hoc and robust initiatives as one of the key parameters for the initiative's start, which remains influential throughout the delivery.

The second part of the book describes common characteristics of analytics initiatives that we can encounter everywhere, like the data-driven approach, technology mix, prototyping and experimentation, etc. These common attributes can impact your analytics initiatives and represent common risks on our analytics journey. We dedicate a large portion of this part to different WoWs as we believe good WoW is one of the critical parameters for managing your analytics for success. We use typical analytics initiatives and demonstrate different WoW for them. We know that the WoW for analytics initiatives is quite different from what we know for application-oriented projects or software-oriented development, and it is more than clear that the right WoW could mitigate many risks and potential challenges. This part describes the challenges that the industrialization of ad-hoc projects can bring and situations arising from how analytics initiatives change over time – time impact. Finally, in this part, we touch on the more applied field, and we show typical analytics initiatives like building complex reporting or delivering AA projects. Using practical and typical situations, we evaluate each project type according to risk factors with descriptions of where and how these situations can affect analytics delivery and how to avoid them.

Thus, we present you with a complex view of analytics initiatives and describe the possible ways to deal with the complexity and analytics initiatives' specifics. It is by no means an exhaustive list of all possible factors (or combinations of factors), and in general, we are not going deep into the details of any of the ideas. Moreover, we do not cover any specific technology, even though it can be crucial for success in analytics projects. We think that a dedicated publication could be written about every single concept mentioned in this book. If we started to consider the technological implications, there would be even more ideas to write down (and we believe that such books are already available). However, this was not the goal of this book.

Our goal was to provide you with a cookbook, teaching you how to think about ANY analytics project in ANY environment. Like in a cookbook, we just want to ensure that you do not skip any crucial "ingredients". Or at least ingredients that are usually used and considered typical. In the end, it is entirely up to you whether you want to include each aspect or not. After all, you know your "taste" best.

You are the one who knows the specific situation well, making you the most competent person to decide what is important. This is true on the project level, department level, company level, and even market level. So feel free to skip any part of the evaluation or add additional criteria. From our perspective, it may be safer to use everything mentioned in the book (which we think are the essentials), but some of it may not necessarily make sense under some circumstances.

What could have a significant impact is the size and type of the company as well. A minor consideration for one company could be huge for another – from all perspectives (all axes). For example, reporting tools will probably exist in big companies (sometimes even more than one), but the standard office toolset could be the only option for small companies. So as always, we need to evaluate and "translate" the requirements based on the right perspective.

We have also tried to highlight what is specific for the analytics/data-driven projects. Understanding these specifics could be the key last (or maybe first) step to a successful analytics project. People working in specific delivery roles usually understand these specifics – albeit sometimes only from a limited perspective. If the management of the project show that they are aware of these aspects and if these are reflected in daily work, it could help with daily delivery. It will build trust that is crucial to high-performance teams.

We hope that you enjoyed the reading. And we wish you all the success on your analytics journey!

Index of Terms

Ad-hoc project:
An ad-hoc project is defined as a one-time effort. There is no expectation that the activity will be repeated or that there will be any savings when repeated. Or, the analytical approach could be used repeatedly, but it is still not worth automatizing it, regardless of whether it is due to the complexity, frequency, or inability to automatize.

Simply said, the automation of repetition does not make any economic sense (however, the end-user would quite often like to do so but cannot find a sponsor for it). There could be several reasons for this:

— The frequency of repetition is too long
— Conditions (inputs for analysis) are changing too quickly
— Automation itself is complex and expensive
— The goal of the activity is to evaluate the approach first and then decide whether we will go for a robust approach (proof of concept, pilot)

Advanced Analytics (AA):
The analytics discipline uses mathematical and statistical calculations to predict the future, predict probability, automate decision processes, or support decision-makers by computation driven results, using analytics models that are first trained and then deployed to real processes. Typical tasks use segmentation, classifications, correlation, or forecast.

Agile:
Agile is an incremental and iterative approach for project development, allowing changes at any time and phase of the implementation (often iterations with business and stakeholders), relying mainly on flexibility and aligning stakeholder needs and company goals.

Analytics landscape:
The analytics landscape is even bigger than a solution (Figure 7.1). It includes a softer definition: the analytics maturity of stakeholders, the company, or even the market. It could also be defined as the readiness to accept the results of analytics and drive the department/business strategy based on the results safely.

Analytics solution (service):
An analytics solution is bigger than just a project or it refers to a coherent activity. Usually, it consists of more than one analytical approach that needs to fit together. For example, sales prediction and reporting define an analytics solution together.

Both could be delivered separately (as a separate project), but both need to consider a wider concept (the concept of the solution). An analytics solution could be very complex and could cover many separate pieces. It is realized in accordance with the agreed terms of the trade and technical specifications.

An analytics product is just a different way to look at this – this time, from a consumer perspective. However, we are taking the delivery team perspective, so we are using terminology like "project" or "solution".

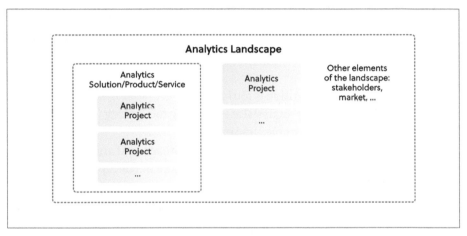

Figure 7.1: The relationship of analytics projects, analytics solutions, and the analytics landscape

Data Analytics Project:
It could be challenging to define the data analytics project in general. From some perspective, every project tries to improve the decision-making process (which could be one high-level definition of analytics). It may focus on the access to information (portal solution) for better decisions, collaboration toolset implementation (to gain quicker access to information over community), or improving any business process (as you would like to gain the results of the process faster). Our definition is stricter. A data analytics project is trying to improve decision processes by bringing or creating insight from data. No matter what type of insight is considered, data need to be the foundation of bringing this insight to the end-user. There could be several ways to improve a decision-making process:

— Create additional insight
— Automatize insight or the decision-making process (to some extent)
— Reduce the time needed to gain the insight

As mentioned, basically every project has an analytical part. For example, projects focusing on business process management (for example, improving the process of mortgages) could have analytics components (an analytics model predicting the probability of not following the payment plan) - see Figure 7.2. In such a case, we can use the same approach to decompose bigger initiatives into smaller projects. For example, we can have "creation of a payment prediction model" as a subtask in the overall project plan and leverage the approach described below just for the defined subtask. It is clear that the overall project determines a great deal as this is basically the solution to which we need to adapt (for example, it largely defines the IT landscape of the analytics tasks).

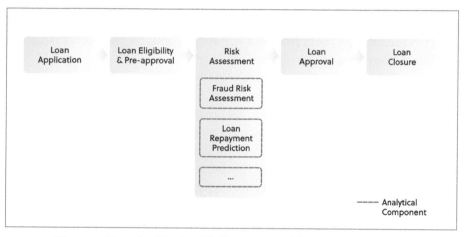

Figure 7.2: Example of the simplified loan process with analytical components

Data discovery:
Data discovery is a business user data-driven process for detecting patterns, gaps, outliers, or insight by visually navigating data. A typical data discovery process contains data preparation, data visualisation, and some advanced analytics principles and functions.

Data engineer:
A data professional with the experience and responsibility to prepare data for analytical needs. They typically create data pipelines to extract, transform, and load data. They might also do data modelling and create data structures in which data are stored.

Data professional:
A person with data analytics skills participating in the delivery of a data analytics project. This includes data analysts, data modellers, data engineers, visualization specialists, or data scientists.

Industrialization:
The work that needs to happen to move from an ad-hoc solution to a robust solution. This work could take many different shapes and could be much more demanding than the original project.

IT platform:
Tools and services offered in the company by central teams (e.g., CoE) with ensured technical support, standards, governance etc., available for multiple internal teams. Examples: A data visualization platform offering modern BI tools, a metadata platform offering a metadata tool with methodologies for data governance, an advanced analytics platform for the deployment of statistical models, their governance and lifecycle management etc.

Project:
The project is a time-limited initiative. We can define it as one step on the analytics journey that can be defined separately, but it needs to fit into the bigger analytics landscape/solution. So, the project could be delivered as a separate activity (from many perspectives: time, finance, team...), but it needs to be delivered in the context of the analytics landscape/solution (as this analytics landscape/solution determines the conditions for successful implementation).

Project Time Frame:
Ad-hoc x robust project feature – based on the definition of the time scope of how long the analytics solution should be in place (see the definition of robust).

Reporting:
Reporting presents and provides operational and financial data to support business decisions, support decision-makers, or refer requested information to regulators. Reporting is provided on an ad-hoc or regular basis, usually to more than one consumer (typically to specific people from management or employees from the distribution network).

Robust project:
A robust project is used to design and implement a repeated, reusable solution (service). The main goal is to have a solution that is scalable, reusable, and automated. Automation means removing manual effort as much as possible (so it saves costs and time). Reusability is defined as the repeated use of analysis over time. Scalability can also have a number of dimensions – the number of users, volume of data, or performance. Usually, we do not need to prove the value of the analytics solution as this is done in the ad-hoc activity (or in any other possible way, for example, by the stakeholders' decision).

Self-Service:
A set of mainly self-explanatory tools and concepts which provides self-sufficiency in the whole data analysis discipline as much as possible. This consists of data preparation, data pipelines, data models, and data visualizations for business users (not often and necessarily developers) without the necessity of technical experience.

Squad:
The basic unit of team organization within agile development. All members of such a team have the necessary knowledge and form an autonomous unit. The result of the squad team's work is always a part of the analytics for individual iterations, which have the task of delivering.

Type of Analytics:
Categorization of the project based purely on the analytical work that needs to happen (descriptive, predictive, cognitive).

Waterfall:
Waterfall is a linear and sequential approach for project development, consisting of defining all requirements at the beginning (avoiding scope changes), implementing them, testing, and deploying to production. This type of development is suitable for straightforward use cases, repeating cases enhancing existing solutions, or cases supported by strong stakeholder maturity.

Way of Working (WoW):
The way the project/work (in our case based on analytics) is being delivered. It covers many aspects, including project delivery methodology, the team's structure, the way the team interacts with other teams, or the ratio between experimentation work and well-defined work.

Index